Woman in the Crested

Woman in the Crested Kimono

The Life of
Shibue Io
and Her Family
Drawn from
Mori Ōgai's
'Shibue Chūsai'

Edwin McClellan

Yale University Press
New Haven and London

Designed by Sally Harris
and set in Galliard type by
Brevis Press, Bethany, CT
Printed in the United States of America by
Vail-Ballou Press, Inc., Binghamton, N.Y.

Library of Congress Cataloging in Publication Data

McClellan, Edwin, 1925–
    Woman in the crested kimono.

    Bibliography: p. 179
    Includes index.
    1. Shibue, Io, 1816–1884.   2. Wives—Japan—Biography.
3. Mothers—Japan—Biography.   4. Shibue, Chūsai, 1805–
1858.   5. Physicians—Japan—Biography.   6. Shibue family.
I. Mori, Ōgai, 1862–1922.   Shibue Chūsai.   II. Title.
CT1838.S517M38   1985   952'.025'0922 [B]   85–5359
ISBN 0–300–03484–9 (cloth)
        0–300–04618–9 (pbk.)

10 9 8 7 6 5 4

To Rachel, Andrew, and Sarah

Contents

Acknowledgments

I am deeply indebted to Koizumi Kōichirō of Tōkai University, on whose scholarly edition of *Shibue Chūsai* I have depended for much of the information in this book. Personally, also, he has been very kind.

Kasaya Kazuhiko of the National Institute of Japanese Literature taught me a great deal about matters relating to domains of the Tokugawa period. I am grateful to him for his constant readiness to help and for his friendship.

Richard Torrance, graduate student at Yale, did a vast amount of research for this book. I cannot thank him enough for his assistance, advice, and companionship as I was writing the final manuscript.

Ken Ito, formerly a graduate student at Yale and now teaching at the University of Michigan, was extremely helpful in the early stages of my work. The research he did then remained invaluable throughout.

Kyoko Lipson, a graduate student at Yale, also gave me invaluable assistance.

When my manuscript was half finished I showed it to Ellen Graham of Yale University Press. Her encouragement and very perceptive suggestions then and later, I shall always be grateful for. It has also been a great pleasure for me to work with Michael Joyce, manuscript editor at the Press.

Rachel McClellan, my wife, as usual helped me more than she knows. A thorough reader and critic, she constantly offered honest and pertinent advice on matters of style and content. Without her generous participation, the book would have suffered from many more infelicities than it now does. She also prepared the index.

Finally, the research fund made available to me through Yale by the Sumitomo group greatly facilitated my work. I wish to express my gratitude now to both Sumitomo and Yale.

The device incorporated into the design of the chapter titles is the Yamanouchi family crest.

A Note on Japanese Names

All the names are given in the Japanese order, surname first.
Mori Ōgai is referred to throughout as Ōgai. This is because
in Japan, when an author adopts a pen name, as in the case of
Ōgai, it normally replaces the given name, while the surname is
retained, and the custom is then to refer to him by his full name
("Mori Ōgai," or "Natsume Sōseki") or simply by his pen name
("Ōgai" or "Sōseki"), but not by his surname alone.

The reader may find Ōgai's, and my, constant use of given
names strangely out of keeping with the formality of the people
and times being described. But while in Japan given names are
used far less frequently in society than they are here, there is no
departure from custom and no suggestion of familiarity in Ōgai's
use of them as a writer referring to persons of the past. Besides,
the persons are more easily distinguishable when identified by
their given names.

After the Meiji Restoration of 1868, many men changed their
given names, from those that seemed too elaborate or formal to
those that seemed less so. "Yutaka," "Osamu," and "Tamotsu" are
post-Restoration names of those in this book who are called differently in their earlier years. To avoid unnecessary confusion, I
have simply used their "modern" names throughout. For the benefit of those who read Japanese and may wish to refer to Ōgai's
book, however, I should add that Yutaka is Yasuyoshi, Osamu is
Senroku, and Tamotsu is Shigeyoshi.

The Principal Characters

The Shibue Family

Shibue Tadashige (1764–1837), Chūsai's father.

Shibue Nui, née Iwata (1775–1829), Chūsai's mother.

Shibue Chūsai (1805–58).

Shibue Sada, née Ojima (1807–?), Chūsai's first wife, divorced 1829.

Shibue Tsuneyoshi (1826–54), son of Chūsai and Sada, Chūsai's initial heir.

Shibue Ino, née Hirano (1806–31), Chūsai's second wife and Sadakata's sister.

Shibue Toku, née Okanishi (d. 1844), Chūsai's third wife.

Shibue Yutaka (1835–83), son of Chūsai and Toku, adopted into the Yajima family in his youth.

Shibue Io, née Yamanouchi (1816–84), Chūsai's fourth wife.

Shibue Tō (1845–51), daughter of Chūsai and Io.

Shibue Kuga (1847–1921), daughter of Chūsai and Io, Yakawa Bun'ichirō's wife.

Shibue Miki (1853–1901), daughter of Chūsai and Io.

Shibue Osamu (1855–1908), son of Chūsai and Io.

Shibue Tamotsu (1857–1930), son of Chūsai and Io, Chūsai's heir.

The Yamanouchi Family

Yamanouchi Chūbei (d. 1839), Io's father.

Yamanouchi Kumi (?1793–1817), Io's mother.

Yamanouchi Eijirō (1812–55), son of Chūbei and Kumi.

Yamanouchi Yasu (1815–76), daughter of Chūbei and Kumi, Nagao Sōemon's wife.

Yamanouchi Io, daughter of Chūbei and Kumi. See Shibue Io.

Maki (1790–1866), Chūbei's mistress.

Nagao Yasu. See Yamanouchi Yasu.

Nagao Sōemon (1814–58), Yasu's husband.

The Yajima Family

Yajima Yutaka. See Shibue Yutaka.

Yajima Tetsu (1846–?), Yutaka's wife.

Yajima Shūtei (1817–?), Yutaka's successor as head of the Yajima house.

Connections

Mori Kien (1807–85), scholar and doctor, friend of the Shibue family.

Hirano Sadakata (1812–76), brother of Chūsai's second wife, Ino, and Io's foster brother.

Shioda Ryōsan (1837–?), Yutaka's friend.

Yakawa Bun'ichirō (1843–?), Kuga's husband.

The Tsugaru House

Tsugaru Yasuchika (1765–1833), ninth lord of the Tsugaru domain.

Tsugaru Nobuyuki (1800–62), tenth lord.

Tsugaru Yukitsugu (1799–1865), eleventh lord.

Tsugaru Tsuguakira (1840–1916), twelfth lord.

Prologue

One of the most admired, though by no means most read, works in modern Japanese literature is an erudite biography of a scholar-doctor named Shibue Chūsai (1805–58) by Mori Ōgai (1862–1922), a senior medical officer of the Japanese army and a towering literary figure of his time. It is from this book that my portrait of Shibue Io (1816–84), Chūsai's wife, is derived.

The reader may wonder why I did not simply translate *Shibue Chūsai*. There are several reasons why I did not: one is that it is so full of esoteric detail—which even the educated Japanese reader finds daunting—that I could hardly expect the lay Western reader to tolerate it in its entirety; another is that though its intended main subject was indeed Chūsai, what I find most interesting is Ōgai's account of Io's life, and I very much wanted to present that to the Western reader, giving it a continuity and emphasis it does not have in the original; and another is that I wanted to incorporate in my narrative, which contains a great many selected passages translated from the original, comments of my own, in the hope that they would add to the reader's understanding not only of Io and other persons connected with her, but of the society and times they lived in, and perhaps also of Ōgai himself, whom I admire.

While so much of Ōgai's book is immensely learned, the parts relating to Io are often simple anecdotal accounts recorded by her son Tamotsu (1857–1930) mostly for Ōgai's benefit, accounts whose veracity cannot be confirmed by diaries, letters, or other written documents. Moreover, Tamotsu was barely one when his father Chūsai died, and was born when his mother was already forty-one, so that he did not witness many of the incidents that he described, but was told about them later by others, including his mother. What Ōgai got from him, therefore, was a combination of family lore concerning Io in her earlier years and personal memories of her in her later years.

There is no question that Ōgai trusted Tamotsu, and his own telling of Io's life varies little from the accounts given him by her son, except of course in style and implicit interpretation. Tamotsu seems to have had an unusually good memory, and very rarely has he been found to have made mistakes in matters that are verifiable. Often he is uncertain about exactly when an incident took place, and when he is, he says so. Sometimes he makes minor mistakes in his reference to the greater events surrounding an incident he is describing, but such mistakes do not affect seriously the significance of the incident itself.

Of course, Tamotsu's memory was not all that he—and Ōgai, for that matter—relied upon. There were, after all, family registers, household accounts and the like that were available to Tamotsu and Ōgai, even if most of Chūsai's notes and journals were lost after the Meiji Restoration of 1868 and little of biographical interest was left in Io's hand. There was Io's daughter Kuga (1847–1921), ten years older than her brother Tamotsu, who gave Ōgai her own account. And then there were descendants of those people who had known Chūsai and Io, with their family records and lore. It was not as though Tamotsu's accounts of Io existed in some sort of vacuum, therefore.[1]

That Ōgai himself, so well acquainted with customs and manners of the Tokugawa period (1603–1867), utterly believed in the reality of Io as she emerged from the various accounts he was given is reflected in the cumulative persuasiveness of his book, which has a consistency of commitment, a solemnity of purpose,

an austere dignity of style, that can only have come from his
conviction of the worthiness of the endeavor. Perhaps the most
elegantly written of all his books, it is almost entirely devoid of
affectation and ornamentation. (There are lapses, to be sure,
which I shall try not to ignore.) It is a book written by a modern
Japanese in his later years—Ōgai was fifty-four when he finished
it in 1916 and was to die six years later—for whom the past has
become terribly important. And a part of his understanding of
the past, of his identification with it, is his dedication to the
person of Io. Such dedication of course has its traps, and Ōgai
does occasionally fall into them; but it does carry authority with
it, too.

An interesting thing about Ōgai's fascination with Io is that he
did not begin his book with her in mind at all. It was Chūsai
who interested him initially, and it was while writing his biography of the man, as more information about the Shibue family
came to him from Tamotsu, that Io became more and more his
preoccupation. Neither Ōgai nor Tamotsu, then, originally intended that she should in any way overshadow her husband; neither, therefore, had a heroine in mind, a heroine who from the
outset had a predetermined role in the book. That Ōgai was
disposed to like and admire a woman like Io, there is no question.
But such disposition surely is a prerogative of any biographer.

Mori Ōgai was born in 1862 in the provincial castle town of
Tsuwano, the seat of a fairly modest daimyo, or baronial, family
named Kamei; and having come of a long line of hereditary doctors retained by the Kamei, Ōgai too was destined to be a doctor.[2]
At the age of ten he was sent to Tokyo, where his family, itself
somewhat undistinguished and without resources to speak of, had
an influential relation in Nishi Amane (1829–97), an intellectual
and public servant of great prominence, who acted as the boy's
sponsor. Ōgai had already by then shown great promise; and it
is a sign of what was expected of him that when in 1881 he graduated from the medical school of the Imperial University of Tokyo
somewhere in the middle of his class, there was general disap-

pointment. He was not in the best of health at the time of the
final examinations; also, it would appear that he had incurred the
displeasure of the resident German lecturer in medicine. Anyway,
his final place in the class might have played a role in his decision
to enter the army medical corps, which, though respectable
enough as a career choice in those days, was not quite as distinguished as, say, staying on at the university. But the one great
attraction of the army was that Ōgai would have the chance of
going to Germany under its auspices.

Ōgai was duly sent to Germany in 1884. His stay there of four
years was obviously fruitful. His knowledge of German, which
was considerable by the time he left Japan, was perfected during
his stay. He read a tremendous amount while there, in philosophy,
literature, history, not to mention medicine. He studied with
some of the best men in medicine, in Leipzig, Dresden, Munich,
and Berlin; at the universities in these cities he attended lectures
by scholars in other fields; and besides, he seems to have had a
surprisingly active social life. Of course he was helped by the fact
that he was a military officer, albeit of a somewhat peripheral
kind, stationed in a country where the right to don an officer's
uniform was held in high regard. But finally whatever was good
about his experience in Germany was due mostly to his lively
intellect, which gave him a certain self-sufficiency. One doubts
that those other Japanese who did not have his appetite for knowledge, his great capacity for reading, could have had half so sat-
isfying a time in Germany, whatever their status.

But the nice thing is that his being a "dilettante"—a word he
too self-consciously used to describe himself, though not coyly—
did not do his career all that much harm. Inevitably, there were
whisperings amongst his fellow servants of the government about
his reading and scribbling; the fact remains, however, that after
his return to Japan in 1888, his place in the medical corps remained
secure, and he eventually became its senior general. He must have
been a good administrator and adroit enough a politician not to
have had to pay the price of being one of the two most renowned

literary figures of his times, the other being Natsume Sōseki (1867–1916). Not only that, he must also have passed muster as a kind of military man. I find it impossible to imagine him being an effete civilian in disguise and at the same time winning the trust and affection of General Count Nogi, an honest-to-goodness soldier who led the bloody attack on Port Arthur in the Russo-Japanese War. True, General Nogi was a civil man with a touch of the poet in him; but it is equally true that in Ōgai, there was a touch of the austere soldier, or perhaps more than a touch.

Ōgai's career as a writer spanned a period of some thirty years. Had he stopped writing in 1912, his reputation today would have rested on his translations from the German, critical writings, and fiction set in modern times; but it was in that year, when General Nogi committed ritual suicide following Emperor Meiji's death, that Ōgai began consistently to write his now famous works about the past.

Distinguished as some of his "modern" fiction written before these may be, even the best of it tends to suffer from what I guess to be Ōgai's doubts about what he was doing when he wrote it. Unlike Sōseki, his great contemporary, he seems to have lacked faith in the validity of fiction. At any rate, what he seems to have looked for as a writer in his later years is meaning in the Japanese past. It isn't that he was disavowing his modern self—whether that part of him which understood Western science and German aesthetics, or that part of him which was inspired by Western literary realism. Rather, it is as though by reasserting the reality of the Japanese past, he was trying to reassert that part of himself which was simpler, more trusting, indeed less "Western." To what extent he was affected by Nogi's suicide, I couldn't say. As an intensely rational, modern man, he must have been shocked by this anachronistic act of self-immolation, by this extreme expression of devotion to his "lord" on the part of someone who was in his own way as much a part of modern Japan as he was. What we must try to understand is that Nogi's suicide was indeed a betrayal of much of what Ōgai stood for. Yet there was surely a side to Ōgai that would not allow him to regard the incident as simply an aberration, as something that he could detach himself from intellectually, if not emotionally.

It would be too sentimental to see the shift in Ōgai's writing simply as the result of the famous incident. No one so complicated—and cautious—as Ōgai could undergo a change quite so quickly. The inclination to explore the past was always there; and he needed to get away from the kind of writing he had been doing. But at the same time, the connection between Ōgai's sustained interest in the past as a writer and Nogi's suicide was, I think, more than symbolic.

There is much violence in some of his "historical" writings that came before *Shibue Chūsai*. In these the sword is ever present, made all the more frightening by Ōgai's refusal to be mystical about it or to romanticize what the more vulgar writers would call "the samurai code." It is there because it existed and was used, and people died by it. I see not the slightest sign of pornographic infatuation on Ōgai's part with pain or violent death. What I do see is a writer who is trying to understand how men and women of another age could die the way they did, for reasons so alien to the modern, rational mind. If death in the past concerns him, it is because he cannot separate it from the rest of the past he wishes to understand.

Perhaps *understand* is the wrong word; for what is conspicuously missing in these works is overt interpretation. What Ōgai wishes to do, it would seem, is to record seemingly incomprehensible or arbitrary events and actions of the past without questioning their meaning, as if the mere act of retelling them, of describing ritual without delving into its reason, would somehow allow him eventual participation.

Whether these tales of violence of the past acted as catharsis for Ōgai, I do not know; but with *Shibue Chūsai*, he leaves behind both that violence (though not entirely, for how could he, given the times he was writing about?) and the detachment of his stance, and enters the far gentler world of a doctor and his wife, their children, relations, and friends; and as he does so, bares himself, especially through his fondness for Io, as he never has before. He seems here at last to have found his own identity as a writer, perhaps even as a modern Japanese who has come to terms with the past and therefore himself.

Ōgai grew up in a family whose women, namely his grandmother and mother, were rather strong-willed, certainly more forceful than his father, a general practitioner with a personality as modest as his practice. How much this had to do with Ōgai's partiality for the kind of woman Io was, or with the possibility that he saw in Io what he wanted to see in a woman, I cannot say.

He divorced his first wife not long after marriage (at some risk to himself, for she was the daughter of an important naval officer who was also a baron, and his relation and former patron, Nishi Amane, had had a hand in the marriage arrangement), but he got on well enough with his second wife Shige (1880–1936, née Araki), by all accounts an attractive woman. I would add that his children had fond memories of him.

Shige had literary aspirations which were encouraged by him, and some of her work was published in *Subaru* ("The Pleiades"), a magazine with which he was closely associated. Both she and Ōgai's younger sister, Koganei Kimiko (1870–1956) were early supporters of the feminist magazine *Seitō* ("Bluestocking," founded in 1911), which became a target of frequent government suppression. The founder of *Seitō*, Hiratsuka Raichō (1886–1971), who scandalized society with her love affairs and was much vilified by the press, said of Ōgai later that he was less prejudiced than most men of his time.[3] And Higuchi Ichiyō (1872–96), that brilliant writer of short stories who died just as she was beginning to win the recognition she deserved, had in Ōgai one of her staunchest admirers.

Before I begin my narrative, I would like here to provide a little background information for the benefit of the lay reader, in anticipation of some of the questions that may soon arise.

The daimyo, the class to which the masters of the Shibue family belonged, were the military nobility, owing fealty to the Tokugawa house, itself a daimyo family (and therefore primus inter pares) with its seat in Edo (renamed Tokyo in 1868). As Shogun, the Tokugawa had ruled Japan since 1603. But in Kyoto, where the Emperor lived in some obscurity, there was the other aristocracy, the *kuge* (or the "civil" aristocracy, as opposed to the "military"), relatively poor and insignificant even before the rise of the Tokugawa, but possessing ancient lineages coveted by the daimyo. Shibue's lords, the Tsugaru, for example, who were among the older of the daimyo families, were thought well-connected mostly because of ties through marriage with very blue-blooded kuge houses.

Apart from those daimyo houses which were officially designated branches of the Tokugawa house, there were two large groupings of daimyo, one called *fudai,* or "inside," and the other called *tozama,* or "outside," each subdivided by degrees of importance, principally according to size of domain. Roughly speaking, the "inside" lords were those whose ancestors had fought under the Tokugawa banner before the Tokugawa ascendancy, and the "outside" lords were those whose ancestors had not declared fealty to the Tokugawa until after.

It was in the name of the Emperor that, more than 250 years after the establishment of the Tokugawa Shogunate, forces now antagonistic to it, led by the great "outside" domains of Satsuma and Chōshū, brought about its downfall and set up a new government under Emperor Meiji in 1868. This great upheaval is what is known as the Meiji Restoration, which marks the emergence of Japan as a modern nation-state.

The Tsugaru were "outside" lords; and though "outside" lords were not by definition antagonistic to the Shogunate, the Tsugaru were not atypical in their ambivalent feelings toward it, and immediately before the Restoration, tended very much to vacillate in the civil war.

In service to the daimyo were the retainers, ranging from the uppermost level of the samurai or *bushi* class, who constituted what one might call the minor military aristocracy, through the horse-owning lesser military gentry, down to those who were at most foot soldiers and who in the stricter domains were not considered bushi at all, though in common usage the term *samurai* seems now to be often applied to them also.

When Shibue Chūsai died in 1858, the Tokugawa political and social system was still in place, though not as firmly as before. He was therefore a person entirely of the Tokugawa period. But Io, who outlived him by twenty-six years, lived through the upheaval and into Japan's "modern" age.

1   The Early Life and Times of Shibue Chūsai

Born in 1805 into a family of hereditary doctors retained since the eighteenth century by the lords of Tsugaru (the northernmost domain on the main island), Shibue Chūsai was distinguished enough to be appointed to the faculty of Seijukan, the Shogunate-sponsored medical school in Edo, at the age of thirty-nine, and later to be presented to the Tokugawa Shogun at the age of forty-four. Ōgai tells us that being appointed to Seijukan was like being appointed to the medical school of the University of Tokyo in his own time. As for being presented to the Shogun, I would suggest that it was comparable to an Englishman in one of the learned professions being given a knighthood today.

But Chūsai's distinction, or reputation, was of that kind which does not survive much beyond the life of the person. Although he was apparently a fine doctor of the traditional, or Chinese school of medicine, as opposed to the Western, or "Dutch" school ("Dutch" because after the closing of Japan to foreigners in the early years of the Tokugawa period, the Dutch, given special concessions, became the main carriers of Western knowledge), and being of the elite of that traditional school, was an accomplished Chinese scholar (he had to be to read ancient Chinese texts with authority), by Ōgai's time his was not a name known except by the most diligent of bibliographers. A minor treatise on the treatment of smallpox, a posthumously published bibliography on Sung and Yuan texts extant in Japan which he co-authored with his friend Mori Kien (1807–81), and a *nagauta* (a sustained lyrical song accompanied by samisen music) published under an assumed name—these constitute his list of publications. This fact of course is no reflection on Chūsai's distinction during his lifetime. After all, publishing was not exactly an activity held in high regard for its own sake in those days among scholars such as Chūsai, much of whose professional scholarly effort was put into careful reading and editing of ancient texts.[1]

Ōgai's interest in him, then, came about by mere chance. Himself a keen antiquarian and collector of old reference books, maps, and such like, his curiosity was aroused when, noting Chūsai's seal and marginal notes in some old *bukan* (registries of noble military houses and important Shogunate officials)[2] that had come into his possession, he became aware of this man of another generation who had shared his innocent passion; and as he began to make tentative inquiries into the identity of Chūsai, his interest in him grew, for he found other traits in him that he either shared or admired.

Like himself a doctor and scholar, holding a high official position; a lover of the serious arts, such as painting, calligraphy, poetry, and the nō, but also an urbane connoisseur of the popular arts, such as kabuki and fiction; a man of discipline and sobriety, yet a loyal and generous friend to men of conspicuous levity; a man recognized for his learning, yet a simple and unaffected man, who would rush out of his house to watch a daimyo procession because he had a childish love of pomp—such is how Chūsai emerges as Ōgai learns more and more about him.

That Ōgai came to like and respect Chūsai cannot have been sufficient reason for writing his book. Rather, I think, it was that through Chūsai, a man of great civility, he could write about a way of life that had passed with the coming of the industrial age in Japan and had never been his own.

Besides, in the end, Chūsai is too nice, too reasonable, to capture our imagination, or indeed to have captured Ōgai's. And if it had not been for Io, the book would never have become the monumental book that it is.

Although highly respected retainers of the Tsugaru lords, the Shibue, being scholar-doctors and not hereditary samurai, were only peripherally of the bushi class, or military gentry. There was a time when medical families would clearly have been denied any claim to membership in that class, but by Chūsai's time, when class distinctions of the finer sort were becoming blurred, a family such as the Shibue, retainers of a daimyo for generations, were de facto bushi.[3]

The Shibue were Edo-based, as opposed to those retainers who were based in Hirosaki, an inland castle town and domainal seat of the Tsugaru lords. Required, with modifications, by the To-kugawa Shogunate to spend every other year in Edo away from their respective castle towns, the daimyo typically maintained three mansions in the city—the upper, the middle, and the lower—and large contingents of retainers, most of whom were not only based in Edo, but like the Shibue, born there.

The hereditary stipend of the Shibue, expressed as was the custom in terms of *koku* of rice, was 300 koku, which put them firmly in the middle stratum of the domainal bushi hierarchy.[4] The Tsugaru themselves were lords of a domain assessed at 100,000 koku.[5] They were by no means "ducal," in the sense that the Shimazu, the Maeda, or the Date were. (The Maeda domain, for example, was assessed at over 1,000,000 koku, and the Date at over 600,000.) But they were hardly lordlings either (daimyo started at 10,000 koku), and among the 265 or so daimyo at the time, they would have been regarded as domainal chiefs of real substance, and were more than usually well-connected.

Chūsai's father Shibue Tadashige (1764–1837) was an adopted son. His true father was a man named Inagaki Seizō, a former bushi of rank who had had to leave his lord's domain after a quarrel with him, and had become an innkeeper in Edo. Tada-shige's adoptive father, Shibue Honkō (1727–84) did indeed have a natural son born to a concubine, but this boy was not thought talented enough to succeed Honkō—his illegitimacy would not have helped his candidacy either—and so Tadashige was chosen.

We shall encounter several more instances of adoption in the course of this narrative. A widely practiced custom throughout the Tokugawa period, its main function was to maintain the continuity of houses and to assure their prosperity. Male adults were constantly being adopted by families which had no sons or, if they did, had none deemed suitable to be head of the household. Male blood relations were often chosen, but blood kinship was by no means a requirement for adoption, and there was no feeling of unnaturalness about the family name and the responsibility of managing the property being inherited by a male who had married into the family. A very common phenomenon of the times—and much later—was the "adopted husband," a male adult who married a daughter of a family and assumed her name and the headship of her natal family. That such a man was often not in an enviable position, any more than a woman marrying into a man's family, one can imagine. Younger sons, of course, were commonly candidates for adoption into other families, though the alternative of establishing their own cadet branches was a possibility. Adoption in Japan, then, was not quite what it has been in the United States or in Britain, where it has tended to be associated with foundlings and charity, and perhaps a certain secretiveness, and has carried emotional overtones absent in the Japanese custom.

Another function that the custom in Japan seems to have served is the diminishing of large families, and the curbing of the necessity on the part of women to go on bearing children until a suitable male heir was produced.[6]

Tadashige had in early boyhood already shown great promise. Had his father Seizō not come down in the world, he would not have considered giving him away for adoption by the Shibue; for the Inagaki had been senior retainers of the lords of Toba, also named Inagaki; but he was now an innkeeper, and of course his talented son would fare better if adopted into a well-established professional family.

To the Shibue, the arrangement was equally acceptable. Had Seizō been forced to flee his lord's domain because he had done something shameful, it would have been a different matter. But an honest argument with his lord, though perhaps ill-advised, showed a certain integrity; and the son of such a man would have been brought up properly. Tadashige therefore had breeding besides intelligence to recommend him.

Shibue Honkō had no surviving daughter whom Tadashige would by custom have married, so that Tadashige's son Chūsai had not a drop of Shibue blood in him.

Tadashige was fourteen when he was adopted. He immediately became a favorite of Nobuakira, two years his senior and later the eighth lord of Tsugaru. This Nobuakira died in 1791 at the age of twenty-nine, and was succeeded by Lord Tsugaru Yasuchika. Yasuchika, then twenty-six, also took to Tadashige, and they became close friends. It was a friendship that lasted until Yasuchika's death in 1833 at the age of sixty-eight. Tadashige died four years later, at the age of seventy-three.

Tadashige was a large man, extremely handsome and much admired by the women who served in the main Tsugaru mansion in Edo. However, we are told, he was not given to flippant ways (though very urbane and not a prude), and behaved with the utmost propriety toward them. And this nice mixture of urbanity and austerity of behavior, his son Chūsai seems to have inherited besides the good looks and intelligence.

The friendship between Tadashige, a doctor and classical scholar placed somewhere in the middle of the bushi hierarchy of the domain, and his lord is entirely plausible. That the relationship would have been very formal by our standards is beyond question, and Tadashige would not have dreamed of taking liberties. But what would have helped their friendship, apart from Tadashige's good looks and poise, was the fact that as a "professional" man, Tadashige was not truly of the military class. True, he represented one of the ideals of that class—Confucian learning and the probity and wisdom associated with it—not to mention the usual sense of awe and dependence a doctor inspires in another, but finally he was an outsider, a gentleman cleric, so to speak, who could cross the dividing lines of rank more easily than a real bushi *because* he was slightly déclassé.

Tadashige married his first wife in 1789. She died the following year. He married again in 1791, but divorced his second wife in 1795, and in the same year married a woman named Iwata Nui (1775–1829) from a bushi family serving Lord Hotta of Sakura Castle. Their first child, a daughter whom they named Suma, was born in 1802. This daughter died in 1826. Their second child, Chūsai, was born in 1805. Tadashige was then forty-one and Nui thirty. Another child, a daughter, was born to them some six years later, but she died in infancy.

We know little about Chūsai's mother Nui—what her role was in his life, what her relationship with her husband was like. She became a lay nun when she was forty-nine, five years before she died. This would suggest a condition of melancholy resignation, but one can hardly conjecture more.

As might be expected, Tadashige saw to it that his son was given the best education that could be had in Edo. At the age of four Chūsai became a pupil of Ichino Meian (1765–1826), a distinguished scholar of the Kōshōgaku school, which emphasized the systematic, empirical approach, as opposed to the highly speculative, in their reconstruction of ancient Chinese texts.[7] After Meian's death, he was taken on by an even more accomplished scholar of the same school, Kariya Ekisai (1775–1835). That at first the teaching and learning would have been of a rather mechanical sort (memorization, reading aloud, and so on), and presumably under Meian's supervision only in the most formal sense, one can imagine. But it is impressive nevertheless that by the time he became Ekisai's pupil at the age of twenty-one, Chūsai had already been studying classical Chinese formally for seventeen years. His medical studies were begun when he was nine, under the tutelage of yet another distinguished man, Izawa Ranken (1786–1836), the smallpox specialist.

A few general remarks here about the practice of medicine in Japan at the time might be helpful. The major specialties in Chinese medicine were internal medicine (*naika*), surgery (*geka*), pediatrics (*nika*), obstetrics (*sanka*), acupuncture (*shinka*), gynecology (*fujinka*), ophthalmology (*ganka*), natural pharmacology (*honsōka*), moxa cautery (*kyūka*), dentistry (*kōchūka*), the treatment of smallpox (*tōka*), and osteopathy (*seikotsuka*). As might be expected, the "Basic Way" (*hondō*) of the doctor was internal medicine, and Chūsai was trained and practiced as an internist.[8] However, we do find him later treating an old woman friend suffering from eye trouble; he was also something of an authority on smallpox; and he must have had some claim to being a responsible pharmacologist, for he was one of the few doctors of the Tsugaru domain to have the right to make and sell at great profit a famous restorative medicine of the time known as *ichiryū kintan* (the primary ingredient of which was opium).[9] It must be noted, however, that the secret formula was inherited by him and that after his death we find Io, who was no doctor, making it too.

In Chūsai's youth "Dutch" medicine was not yet the threat to Chinese medicine that it became by the time of his death. More scientific and experimental, far less bound by classical scholarship, it would eclipse Chinese medicine in the latter half of the nineteenth century. But this is not to say that the risk factor for a patient being treated by a doctor of the "Dutch" school in Chūsai's time was necessarily smaller than that for a patient being treated by a traditional doctor.

In such areas as anatomy, surgery, and pathology, the "Dutch" school was unquestionably more advanced. And in the treatment of the most dreaded disease of the time in Japan—smallpox—the practitioners of Chinese medicine were behind. But it is interesting that a form of vaccination against smallpox was known and used in Japan before Jenner's time, though erratically and at more than little risk to the patient—and also infrequently, it would seem, for there is no evidence that Chūsai, for example, used it to protect his children against the disease.[10]

As for the general level of competence of doctors of the Chinese school in their own terms, one could say that those retained by the daimyo or the Shogunate had unquestionably respectable academic pedigrees, though whether their ability as practitioners would necessarily reflect their academic credentials would be another matter. There were also those doctors who did not have official appointments, and among these, whether they practiced in Edo or in smaller towns, there was an enormous variation in competence, ranging from responsible general practitioners to out-and-out quacks. Given the fact that there was no institutionalized system of examination of would-be doctors in Japan, such variation was to be expected.

Chūsai seems to have had no private practice to speak of. Those instances of treatment of private patients by him that we shall encounter were special, occurring only when friends were ill or when charity called. His chief duty as a doctor when he had attained senior rank was to attend to his lord, whose condition he would examine regularly at one of the Tsugaru mansions in Edo. His responsibilities as a doctor, then, were not onerous. And there is no suggestion that he ran any personal risk, bodily or otherwise, if his lord's condition, if unwell, did not improve. One great advantage that such a doctor as Chūsai had was that he had colleagues to share his opinions with, thus avoiding blame for possible misdiagnosis or mistreatment.[11]

One has to remember, however, that he was a scholar and teacher too, and in that capacity, his time was amply employed, though all in all one gathers that he had much free time for leisurely occupations, such as going to parties and the theater, and reading and writing fairly frivolous things.

Apart from his formal studies, there was the society of Edo

literati—classical Chinese and Japanese scholars, theater critics, antiquarians, painters, poets, playwrights, calligraphers—that Chūsai was exposed to as he grew up. A society notable for its sophistication, wit, connoisseurship, tolerance, and easy companionship (and, it must be admitted, gross levity on occasion), it represented, though perhaps in an overripe sense, the very peak of Edo culture. Japan was never to see its like again.

It was a time when different arts and pursuits, which once had been seen as either "popular" (such as kabuki and fiction) or "serious" (such as nō and the study of classics) and had tended to be identified with different classes, could be happily combined in a typically cultivated man of Edo, as they were in Chūsai himself; so that the educated man who held kabuki or fiction in contempt because of their "popularity" would be regarded as something of a boor by the more sophisticated.

It was a time when the writing of poetry in Chinese was enjoying a renaissance; when one of the most famous kabuki actors of all time, Ichikawa Danjūrō VII (1791–1859), was introducing changes that would raise the prestige of kabuki to new heights; when a great amount of popular fiction was being written by some of the best-known names in Japanese literature, whose reading public, consisting of men, women, and children, supported in 1808 over six hundred officially listed lending libraries in Edo; when teachers of calligraphy, of painting, of the classics, of Japanese poetry, and of music flourished as they probably never had done before, and met one another regularly in drawing rooms, theaters, and in restaurants.

It is characteristic of that society that someone like Chūsai, a devoted Confucian scholar, should have loved the theater as he did, and should have written a novel, unpublished and now lost, presumed to have been intended for very light reading; or that his son Tamotsu, brought up to succeed Chūsai as a scholar and doctor, should in his youth have become a fan of sumō wrestling and an avid collector of woodblock prints (a popular art form) without, it would seem, any censure from his family or mentors.

That such blurring of the distinction between the "serious" and the "non-serious," such easy sophistication and love of entertainment—and, inevitably, the extravagance and the irresponsibility that went with it, though certainly not in Chūsai's or his son Tamotsu's case—should have dismayed certain conscientious officials of the Shogunate is not surprising; and during Chūsai's lifetime they made efforts to restrain the activities of some of the more conspicuous purveyors of "moral corruption," such as Danjūrō the actor and several major fiction writers. But it would seem that such attempts at moral reform on the part of the government did not touch deeply either Edo cultural life or the personal social life of a man like Chūsai, who, apart from curtailing his visits to the kabuki theater after having been presented to the Shogun, essentially continued to live as he had done before.[12]

Chūsai was formally presented to his lord, Tsugaru Yasuchika, in 1815 when he was ten years old. After that, so long as he was sufficiently intelligent and educated, and conducted himself properly, he would eventually inherit his father's position; and as was expected, his career progressed satisfactorily. In 1822, at the age of seventeen, he was appointed *goban minarai* (apprentice physician) and *omote isha* (physician of the outer chambers). His duties would have consisted of treating minor emergency cases and attending the sick among the less exalted of Tsugaru retainers. He was then promoted to *kinjū isha suke* (assistant physician to the lord) in 1829; to *kinjū tsume* (associate physician to the lord) in 1836; and finally to full *kinjū* in 1843. A kinjū, whether assistant, associate, or full, would be among those handpicked physicians of the domain who would attend the lord and his immediate family.

When Tsugaru Nobuyuki retired as the tenth lord and moved to the lower Tsugaru mansion in Edo, Chūsai was "seconded" to him as *inkyo-zuke* (physician to the retired lord). This was in 1839, when Chūsai was still an associate kinjū. Chūsai's being assigned to duty at the lower mansion would of course suggest his closeness to the retired lord; but what it meant also was that he was being removed from duty at the upper mansion, now the residence of Tsugaru Yukitsugu, the eleventh lord. He would report to the upper mansion from time to time; but he had in effect been removed from the center of official domainal life in Edo. The removal seemingly did not affect Chūsai's career in any noticeable way, however. Certainly he did not sink into obscurity afterward. One advantage of the hereditary system—at least from the point of view of someone like Chūsai—was that his association with Nobuyuki, whose retirement took place rather early in his life and therefore presumably under a cloud (he was rumored to be extravagant), did not prevent him from attaining the highest domainal rank as a doctor. Four years after Nobuyuki's retirement, he was promoted to full kinjū. And then, a year later, he was appointed to the faculty of the Seijukan, the Shogunate-sponsored medical school.[13]

The appointment was greeted with some reservation by Lord Tsugaru Yukitsugu and the senior domainal retainers. An appointment to the Shogunate's medical school of one of their physicians was an honor not to be refused without giving offense. On the other hand, the Tsugaru were by this time—perhaps always—ambivalent in their attitude toward the Shogunate, watchful of indications of the waning of Tokugawa power, jealous of their own autonomy, and not anxious to see any of their retainers acquire connections with the Tokugawa, no matter how remote. And so permission was given Chūsai to accept the appointment, with more than a hint that it was at best a mixed blessing in the eyes of his lord.

Chūsai married for the first time in 1824, at the age of nineteen. He had the previous year inherited the headship of his family, his father having retired at the age of fifty-nine. The woman he married was named Ojima Sada, daughter of a *rōnin*, or bushi without a lord, and therefore without proper employment. It was not exactly a misalliance—after all, Chūsai's grandfather had been a rōnin turned innkeeper—but Chūsai could have married a woman from a more prosperous family. The reason for the choice, we are told, was that a woman who had known poverty was thought likely to be able to manage the household with sense and frugality. Sada, however, failed to live up to expectations; and in 1829 Chūsai divorced her. They had one son, named Tsuneyoshi, born in 1827. Soon after divorcing Sada, Chūsai married Hirano Ino, daughter of Hirano Bunzō, a bushi of the Tsugaru domain. Like the Shibue, the Hirano were Edo-based, their hereditary position being that of *rusui*, or liaison officer. The rusui of the various domains, Ōgai tells us, formed the "corps diplomatique" in Edo, for it was through them that the domains of approximately equal status maintained diplomatic relations with one another, and exchanged information.[14]

We may presume that Chūsai's second marriage was a happy one. But soon after giving birth to a daughter, Ino died. This was in 1831, only two years after she and Chūsai were married. The daughter, named Ito, died in 1850 at the age of nineteen.

The Shibue and the Hirano remained friends long after Ino's death. This would suggest that Chūsai and Ino were indeed happy in their marriage, or at least that the Hirano had no cause for complaint in Chūsai's treatment of Ino.

Chūsai married again in 1831—the same year that Ino died—this time to the daughter of a fellow doctor, Okanishi Eigen, who was a retainer of Lord Abe of Fukuyama Castle.

Chūsai did not like Toku, his third wife. He knew her brother, whom he liked and respected, and had wrongly imagined, we are told, that she would be like him. Her side of the story, we don't know. At any rate, their relationship had become quite loveless by the time she died, which was in 1844, thirteen years after they were married. She bore three children, only one of whom, a son named Yutaka, born in 1835, survived infancy and grew to adulthood.

And so when Chūsai married Yamanouchi Io, his fourth wife, in 1844, there were three surviving children by his previous marriages: his older son, Tsuneyoshi, aged seventeen; his daughter Ito, aged thirteen; and his younger son, Yutaka, aged nine.

2  The Young Io

This is how Ōgai introduces Io:

'The woman whom Chūsai then took as his wife was Io, of the surname of Yamanouchi. In the years between Chūsai's marriage to Toku and his marriage to Io he had risen in status, and was now an appointee of the Shogunate. With the rise had come greater social obligations and expenses, so that the responsibilities Io had to assume immediately upon becoming the new mistress of the Shibue household were considerable. That at this time of change and difficulty in family circumstances Chūsai should have married a woman of Io's qualities was his good fortune.

'Io's father's name was Yamanouchi Chūbei. . . . A wholesale hardware dealer by trade, he had his residence and his business establishment, which was called Hinoya, in Kon'ya-chō in the Kanda district of Edo. . . . He was a connoisseur of the arts, and liked the society of men of letters and artists. He was indeed a patron of theirs, and spent a great deal of money in their support.

'Chūbei had three children: Eijirō, his son and heir, and two daughters, Yasu and Io. He had been a friend of Tadashige, Chūsai's father, and had for some time entrusted his son's education to Chūsai. It is said that when Io was about eight or nine—that is, 1824 or 1825—she and her sister Yasu, who was a year older, would go into the drawing room whenever Tadashige called on their father, and listen raptly to their elders' conversation about the theater. . . .

'Io was born in 1816, when her elder brother Eijirō was four and her elder sister Yasu was one. Chūbei took great care over the education of all three of his children as each reached the educable age. Eijirō was given an education fit for a gentleman; his daughters, besides being given the standard instruction in reading, writing, and the various ladylike accomplishments, were trained in the martial arts, and when still girls were sent away to serve in daimyo houses [in Io's case, first to Edo Castle, the seat of the Shogun, when terribly young]. Indeed, Io was even given instruction in Confucian studies, almost as though she were a male.

'Their family origin would explain the way in which Chūbei brought up his children. They apparently traced their ancestry back to a younger brother of Lord Yamanouchi Kazutoyo [1546–1605], son of Lord Yamanouchi Moritoyo [1508–57]; and Chūbei's forefathers, even after they had become Edo merchants, continued to use the Yamanouchi crest of three oak leaves and to adopt alternate personal names which contained the character for *toyo*, a character traditionally present in the personal names of Yamanouchi lords.'[1]

Technically, being merchants, Io's family belonged to a class lower in the rigidly defined social hierarchy than the Shibue; and because of this, Io was first formally adopted by Hirano Bunzō, father of Chūsai's late second wife Ino, and then given in marriage to Chūsai as an Hirano. Yet, formalities of social distinction notwithstanding, Io was actually a more "stylish" person than any of Chūsai's earlier wives, indeed more patrician. For though her family were in trade, they were undeniably rich; Chūbei was a generous patron of the arts, Io had been given the best education money could buy (going to serve in daimyo houses is likened by Ōgai to going to a fashionable women's college in his day), and they were proud of their ancestry.

Ōgai sees no reason to doubt Io's family's claim to descent from the Yamanouchi lords, though he fails to determine precisely which "younger brother" had begun the line. And one is inclined to trust his judgment here. There were, it is true, a great many bushi families, including daimyo, in those days with family trees that were highly imaginative. But it was another matter for a merchant family to claim such distinguished ancestry with the conviction shown by Io's family. It is interesting that when the Yamanouchi crest on her dress is challenged by a senior woman retainer at Lord Yamanouchi's upper mansion—it was one of several such interviews she had at the great daimyo houses—Io is not at all intimidated.

In inculcating the ancestral severity and martial spirit in Io, however, her father surely got more than he bargained for:

'[When Io was a child there was a woman living in their house named Maki.] This Maki was born in 1790, and at an early age was hired as a maid by Io's grandmother. In 1803, when she was thirteen, she became the mistress of Io's father Chūbei. When Chūbei later married Kumi, of the house of Yamaichi, paper dealer, Maki was twenty. Kumi was then only seventeen. A beloved child of a rich merchant, she was of a gentle disposition. It was said later that of her two daughters Io and Yasu, the latter, with her withdrawn ways, was more the mother's daughter than her spirited sister. What kind of woman Kumi was, then, is not difficult for us to imagine. On the other hand, while it would seem that Maki was not a particularly aggressive woman, she was after all three years Kumi's senior, and more worldly-wise. We can hardly doubt therefore that Kumi would have found it difficult to exercise authority over Maki, indeed that she would as likely as not have been under the other's control.

'Kumi bore four children—Eijirō, Yasu, Io, and a second son. But immediately after giving birth to this last child she fell ill and died. The child died with her.

'Before she died she had become hard of hearing, perhaps because of some problem with her blood circulation.

'Eijirō was five at the time. And during his mother's confinement, he overheard Maki refer to her as "that deafie." This he never forgot, and when his sister Io was five or six, he told her. Io flew into a rage, and said to her brother: "Maki is our blood enemy, then. You and I will avenge our mother someday, won't we?" Afterward, she would rest a broom upside down against a wall, tie a dusting cloth on it so that the two dangling ends stood for arms, and put some clothes on it. She would then pretend she had a sword in her hands, and bringing it down with great force shout, "Remember what you did to mother!" Both her father and Maki knew whom the little girl had in mind to cut down; but the father had no inclination to have an open row with his daughter, and Maki was too frightened to chide the girl.

'Anxious to foster more friendly feelings in the girl, Maki tried to please her with sweet words, but Io was beyond such enticement. Maki also approached Io's father and suggested that he have the girl call her "Mother," but this Chūbei refused to do. He knew Io's character only too well, and did not wish to risk angering her even more.'²

A few years after this, when Io was ten or eleven, she went to Edo Castle to serve as a junior attendant. Even for those days this was very young for a girl to leave home; and there seems little doubt that it had to do with her dislike of her father's mistress.

In Edo Castle Io apparently was attached to the chief lady-in-waiting at the time, Lady Anekōji of the civil aristocracy, or kuge, from Kyoto. And if indeed Io was attached to this lady, Ōgai tells us quite solemnly, she must have been quartered in the premier section at the southern end of the long row of apartments assigned to ladies-in-waiting at the castle. (The building in which they were quartered, and which was the residence of the Shogun and his family, would more properly be called "the palace," for it was a huge, one-storey mansion standing in the grounds of a great fortress.)

'There was a window far down the corridor running alongside these apartments which the girl attendants had to close every evening. The duty became most unpopular once the rumor began

that a demon lurked about in the corridor. None of the girls had
seen this creature clearly; all that was known was that he was
dressed in man's clothes, had horns growing out of his forehead,
and was in the habit of throwing pebbles and ashes at them as
they walked past. Being plucky by nature and having had some
training in the martial arts, young Io was not so fearful as the
others, and one evening, when they all refused to go, she went
to close the window by herself.

'As she walked down the dark corridor she thought she saw a
figure scurrying towards her. A moment later one side of her face
was covered with ashes. Deciding quickly that this was more like
a boyish prank than the act of any demon, she jumped at the
shadowy figure beside her and got a firm hold of him. "I'm sorry,
I'm sorry!" he cried, struggling to free himself. Io held on to her
prisoner until the other girls came running. The demon finally
surrendered and took off his mask. He turned out to be one of
the Shogun Tokugawa Ienari's younger sons, who went by the
name of Ginnosuke in his youth. . . .'³

It is not known when Io left Edo Castle. But Ōgai's guess is
that since it is known that she began her service at Lord Tōdō's
upper mansion in 1830 when she was fourteen, she probably left
the castle the year before. Ōgai is perhaps hinting that she would
not have stayed at home very long.

'We are told that before going to work for the Tōdō family she
went to over twenty other daimyo houses to be interviewed. It
would seem that like knights of old who chose their lords to serve
under, women like Io seeking employment in the great houses in
those days went to such interviews not so much to be chosen by
their prospective employers as to choose *them*. She had not been
turned down by all these houses, then; rather, we gather, she had
not found them to her liking.

'But there had been one that she thought she could work for;
and this, by sheer coincidence, was the house of Matsudaira To-
yosuke, Lord of Kōchi in Tosa Province, whose real family name
was Yamanouchi and who therefore had ancestors in common
with Io.

'At Lord Yamanouchi's upper mansion in Kajibashi, Io was given the customary examination. The examination, in other words, consisted of tests in calligraphy, writing Japanese poetry in the classical thirty-one-syllable mode, and music. The examiner was a senior woman attendant. An inkstone, a writing brush, and a piece of formal, patterned paper were put in front of Io. "Would you write something on that?" the woman said. Io promptly wrote a poem of her own making, thus passing simultaneously the tests in calligraphy and poetry. She then chanted a ballad of the Tokiwazu school, and the examination was over. The examination itself was no different from those she had been given at the other houses; but what caught her attention in this particular house was the fact that all the women she saw were dressed modestly in cotton clothes. She was pleased by such simplicity in the house of a great daimyo whose domain was assessed at over 240,000 koku, and she decided then and there that this was where she wanted to work. . . .

'Then the woman saw that the small crest imprinted on Io's dress was three oak leaves.

'Why, she wanted to know, was Io wearing the crest of the master's family, the Yamanouchi? Io replied simply that her family's name too was Yamanouchi, and that they had worn the crest for generations. [Presumably, as a daughter of a merchant, she would not have used her surname for the interview, but would have referred to herself as the daughter of "Hinoya," the business name her father would have gone by.]

'After giving the matter some thought the woman then said that she had been favorably impressed by Io and would like to recommend her for appointment; but for the time being at least, would she refrain from wearing the crest? No doubt Io's family had a legitimate, long-standing claim to it, and later, when she had been in service for a while, she could formally request permission to wear it.

'When she returned home Io asked her father what she ought to do: should she, for the sake of working in Lord Yamanouchi's house, make a secret of her crest initially, as the woman had suggested? Absolutely not, said the father: names and crests were sacred things inherited from one's ancestors, and were not to be tampered with lightly. If hiding her crest was the condition of her appointment, she had better refuse it.

'Io accordingly declined the offer from the Yamanouchi house. Her next interview was at the upper mansion of the Tōdō family, situated in Mukō-Yanagihara. She was given the usual examination, which she again passed with ease. This time the offer of appointment was more like an entreaty. They would accord her favored status, they said, so would she come? Pleased by such reception and tired of being interviewed, she decided to accept their offer.

'She was immediately made a *chūrō*, or female attendant of the middle rank, assigned to the lord's quarters, with the additional responsibility of being private secretary to Lady Tōdō. Her master, Tōdō Takayuki, was lord of Tsu in Ise Province, a great domain of over 320,000 koku. . . . Lady Tōdō was a cousin of his, being a daughter of Lord Tōdō Tadatake.

'Io at the time was fourteen, and normally a girl of her age would have been retained as what was then called a "female page," a person who brought in tea, tobacco, washing water, and the like; so that her appointment as a chūrō, that is, as someone who would transmit her master's wishes to female pages, besides being generally useful in his chambers was indeed a departure from custom. . . .

'She was given the personal service name of Kazashi. This was the personal name she was registered under when later it was decided that she would marry Chūsai as an adopted daughter of the Hirano family. But after a while, when it was discovered that she had received training in the martial arts, she came to be referred to in the Tōdō household as "the tomboy."

'As a chūrō Io had an apartment of three rooms, and kept two maids. Her own food and the maids', she herself had to pay for. In these respects, the conditions of her employment were no different from what they would have been in some other daimyo's house. But whereas her yearly salary in another house would have been thirty *ryō* or thereabouts, in the Tōdō house it was only nine.[4]

'The fact is that women serving in military houses as Io did had no expectation of making a lot of money. They were there to be educated. Today, their counterparts would go to women's colleges. For someone like Io, who was careful to choose a household which showed refinement and discipline, salary was never a consideration.

'After all, an education is something one spends money on; going to school is hardly a money-making occupation. We are told that Io's father, Chūbei, spent four hundred ryō a year to enable his daughter to meet her obligations while in service: gifts for the Tōdō officials, entertainment of her colleagues, appropriate clothes and furnishings for herself, the keeping of two maids. Under these circumstances, whether Io was paid thirty ryō or nine could have mattered very little to her or Chūbei.

'Io was much trusted in the Tōdō household. On New Year's Day in 1831, after less than a year's service, she was made the head chūrō. This was a position normally occupied by a woman of twenty-three or -four. Io was then barely fifteen.

'Her service with the Tōdō family lasted nine years. In 1839, at the age of twenty-three, she resigned, giving as her reason her father's illness. During her years of service in Edo Castle and in the Tōdō house, Chūsai, her future husband, had been married three times: to Sada, née Ojima, while Io was at Edo Castle, and to Ino, née Hirano, and to Toku, née Okanishi, while Io was at the Tōdō house.

'The year Io resigned was also the year her father died. But at the time of her resignation Chūbei was not so ill as to require his daughter's immediate return home. The real reason for her resignation was that that year Lord and Lady Tōdō were to go on a pilgrimage to the Grand Shrine of Ise, which was some three hundred miles distant from Edo, and Io had been picked to be a member of the retinue for the long journey. Chūbei simply did not want to see her go, and made sure that she resigned well in advance of her master's departure from Edo.

'Living with Chūbei in the house in Kon'ya-chō at the time of Io's return were his mistress Maki, aged forty-nine, and Io's elder brother Eijirō, aged twenty-seven. Io's elder sister Yasu, aged twenty-four, had four years before left Lord Abe's house where she was serving and married Nagao Sōemon, a wholesale lacquerware dealer in Yokoyama-chō. Sōemon was only one year older than Yasu. . . .

'With the approach of old age Chūbei had become rather weak-willed. As for Maki, she was never the sort that could assume command. Neither, then, was capable of dealing with the very serious problem that the Hinoya establishment was faced with at the time of Io's return. This had to do with the conduct of Io's elder brother Eijirō.

'Eijirō had begun attending Shōheikō, the Shogunate-sponsored college, after having studied for a while under Chūsai's tutelage. There was only one other merchant's son attending the college at the time: this was Sōemon, who later married Eijirō's sister Yasu. The rest were all of bushi rank. To offer a rough analogy, today's counterparts of these two merchants' sons at Shōheikō would be sons of non-titled families attending the Peers' School.

'While Io was in service at the Tōdō house Eijirō became bored with being a student and began visiting Yoshiwara, the pleasure quarter. The woman he went to see there belonged to one of the more elegant brothels, and was called Tsukasa. Two years before Io left service the relationship between these two had reached the point where Eijirō began to think seriously of redeeming Tsukasa [that is, paying the brothel the necessary redemption fee, which would have been a substantial sum, given the elegance of the establishment, and making a respectable woman out of her]. On hearing about this Chūbei said he would disown Eijirō; but thanks to Io, who came to Hinoya to intercede on her brother's behalf and to talk sense into him, the matter was laid to rest.

'But by the time Io resigned her position Eijirō had got himself into trouble again.

'Having been saved by his sister from dire punishment, Eijirō had for a while been the penitent son and not set foot in Yoshiwara. In the meantime Tsukasa was redeemed by some rich fellow from the provinces. This threw Eijirō into a fit of depression. Touched by his son's misery, Chūbei weakly asked an acquaintance to take Eijirō for a visit to Yoshiwara. There Eijirō discovered that Tsukasa's former waiting girl was to "come out" the following month under the professional name of Hamateru. He duly returned to become one of her regular customers. Very soon he was visiting Yoshiwara more often than ever before. Again Chūbei began to threaten Eijirō with expulsion. Then he fell ill. Even Eijirō, it would seem, was chastened by Chūbei's illness, and temporarily restrained himself. It was during this lull that Io returned.

'Io's sister Yasu was a weak and irresolute woman. Yasu's husband Sōemon, ever since he succeeded to the family business after his elder brother's untimely death, had done little but drink and amuse himself. He was not up to managing his own affairs, let alone his father-in-law's. It is not surprising, then, that Io felt compelled to leave the Tōdō house in order to salvage Hinoya's rapidly declining fortunes.

'Io had not only to save singlehandedly a merchant house in disarray from total collapse: there was her enfeebled father to nurse and comfort, a wayward brother to exhort. And again she managed to prevent Chūbei from disowning Eijirō. This time she got Chūbei's elder half-brother, a certain Ōmago who had once served on the ten-man Council of City Merchants, to act as guarantor for Eijirō.

'Chūbei died on January 11, 1840. He had willed all his money to Io [presumably without having formally disowned Eijirō], but she immediately had it put back in her brother's name.

'To say that Io received a man's education is not merely to refer to that martial side of it that earned her the nickname of "the tomboy" at the Tōdō mansion. For in the world outside, she was known as "the new Shōnagon"—"new" because Taka, her contemporary and the daughter of the scholar Kariya Ekisai, was already called "Shōnagon" [after Sei Shōnagon, the famous woman writer of the late tenth and early eleventh century, who was more learned than was sometimes thought good for her].

'We are told that at one time or another she studied Confucianism under Satō Issai [1772–1859], calligraphy under Ubukata Teisai [1799–1856], painting under Tani Bunchō [1763–1840], and Japanese poetry under Maeda Natsukage [1793–1864]. Since she was already in service by the time she was ten or eleven, "studying" with them must have meant going to lectures whenever she had leave to go home, copying calligraphy or composing poetry on a specified subject beforehand and then having her work corrected by her teacher. . . .

'Io married Chūsai five years after leaving the Tōdō house. She had known him since she was a child; but it was only after the death of Chūsai's wife Toku in April of 1844 that the possibility of her marrying him became at all real. For long a frequent visitor at the Shibue house, she visited Chūsai from time to time during the eight months that intervened between Toku's death and her own marriage. This was a time when people did not dream of such a thing as friendship between man and woman before marriage, or marrying someone of one's own deliberate choosing. Yet these two—a strictly educated man of thirty-nine and an equally strictly educated woman of twenty-eight, both in full awareness of what they were doing—were able to transform a friendship of many years' standing suddenly into marriage. It was surely an extraordinary thing to have happened in those days.

'How did they behave toward each other, I wonder to myself, when Io first called on the recently widowed Chūsai to offer her condolences? Probably rather formally and nervously. And I recall with amusement an anecdote which Io later told her son Tamotsu and which he repeated to me. One day not long before they were married she visited Chūsai and was talking to him when Hōkaishi

[1799–1863; theater critic and antiquarian, whose real name was Ishikawa Jūbei] dropped in. He had in his hand a small package wrapped in bamboo sheath which he promptly began to open as soon as he had sat down. Inside were pieces of sushi. "Here, have one," he said to Chūsai as he helped himself. "And you, too," he added, turning to Io.

'When telling this story Io apparently commented that never in her life had she been so embarrassed.'⁵

The sushi would have been of the coarser, "take-out" variety. Anyway, an analogy would be a Victorian lady being presented with fish and chips wrapped in newspaper in the drawing room. Also, her embarrassment would have been partly that she had been found visiting an unmarried man.

I think that Ōgai's telling of Io's and Chūsai's marriage is quite eloquent. I think, too, that behind his admiration for Io's independence there is a sad reminder that such a marriage would have been nearly impossible even in his own time.

Why she waited so long to marry is a question. She had breeding, at least some money, a fine education, and, we are told, good looks. Ōgai is not very explicit about it, probably thinking that the reader's guess would be as good as his own. At any rate, there are likely reasons that come immediately to mind. Most men of her class would have been afraid of her. She was too forceful, too intelligent, and too well-educated. It was one thing to like and admire her, as many men did; it was another to think of marrying her. Her brother Eijirō, her brother-in-law Sōemon, and even her father Chūbei were somewhat in awe of her, and there is no reason to think that other rich merchants and their sons would have felt differently about her. For her part, she could not have relished the thought of marrying a man who, like her father, would make a young maid his mistress, or who, like her brother-in-law, would pass the day in an alcoholic haze, or who, like her brother, would become enraptured with a prostitute. She was no prig; indeed, she was often very good to wayward men. But again, it was one thing to tolerate or even like some of them; it was another to think of marrying one of their kind; and among sons of rich merchants, they seemed to be very numerous.

There was more than sisterly goodwill behind her making sure that Eijirō remained their father's heir. Had she been the heir instead, she would have had to take in an "adopted husband," who because of his status would be subject to interference from Eijirō, the former rightful heir. Much better, then, to leave the house altogether, and marry someone who would command Eijirō's respect.

How many suitors Io had before she married Chūsai, we don't know. We do know of one in particular, and this was the painter Satake Eikai (1803–74). One New Year's Day he called on the Yamanouchi family to pay his respects, and finding Io standing by the pond in the garden went to her side and tried to hold her hand. Io grabbed his hand instead, pulled hard, then let go. Satake fell into the pond. He was given a set of Eijirō's clothes to change into and sent home. Later, after she was married, she happened to come across Satake at a party for literati and painters held at a famous restaurant. Looking at the numerous geishas that surrounded him, she said, "Heroes can't do without their women, as the saying goes."[6]

Chūsai was an attractive man; he was also learned and intelligent, and knew how to behave. He had his disadvantages: he had been married three times before, had children by his previous marriages, and was not rich; but these were outweighed by his personal qualities and professional distinction. Moreover, Io's father and his had been friends, and she had known him for years, ever since she was a child.

As Ōgai nears the end of his book, he discovers that Io was quite aggressive in her pursuit of Chūsai after he had become a widower. Without a touch of coyness, she persuades a mutual acquaintance to act as her go-between. It is to Ōgai's credit that he does not find this shockingly unfeminine.

3 The Family and Friends

There seems little question that Chūsai and Io's marriage was a happy one. Ōgai does not tell us so explicitly. Instead, he simply reports various incidents which in themselves may not be of much significance but suggest a shared tolerance and concern for friends and relations, and absolute trust in each other's standards. They were not exactly alike, of course. Of the two Io was the more headstrong, and Chūsai the more peaceable. Had Chūsai been a true bushi, and therefore perhaps more concerned for his masculinity, the difference might have proved embarrassing. But bushi or no bushi, the fact is that Chūsai's self-regard was not at all threatened by Io's forceful personality. Later, we shall see how much more decisive Io was than her husband in the face of physical danger. But in Chūsai's acceptance of Io's physical courage and in the absence of any suggestion of condescension on Io's part, we see an assurance in both which has little to do with conventional notions of masculinity or femininity.

Love is not a word Ōgai ever uses in his description of the marriage. Partly this is because neither Chūsai nor Io would have dreamed of using such a word to describe his or her feelings for the other. Partly, it is a reflection of Ōgai's own shyness, incongruous by Western biographical standards, about probing too deeply into their feelings. It is the same reticence that later prevents him from using the word *sorrow* when writing about Io after Chūsai's death.

The condition of their marriage, then, is suggested by such innocent anecdotes as the one that follows. It is similar to the one about Hōkaishi and his sushi, in that the quality of Chūsai's and Io's relationship is illustrated by the easiness of another person in their presence. Here, the visitor is Izawa Shinken (1804–52), a scholar-doctor and close friend of Chūsai's.

'Shinken paid little attention to the proprieties. It was his habit to walk straight into the Shibue house and announce himself from outside the drawing room. He would bring with him cooked eel or something of the sort, and ask for rice gruel to go with it. "Pretend I'm not here," he would say to Chūsai, "I've come to talk to your wife anyway." Having thus driven Chūsai away to the study, he would then sit with Io, drinking, eating, and chatting.'[1]

Our preconceptions about Japan in "feudal" times are such that we sometimes are unable to realize how free social life in Edo could be in the first half of the nineteenth century. There were of course formalities to be observed which would be unimaginable in a twentieth-century democratic society. But perhaps because of those formalities, or certainties about rules, we see in Chūsai's circle a tolerance for eccentricity, indeed sometimes for outright impropriety, that is very attractive.

Chūsai's house was always full of staying guests—hangers-on, if you like—who simply came for lack of anywhere else to go. Some were students who tried to make themselves useful around the house in exchange for free board and lodging, some were friends or relations in need of shelter. One of these was Mori Kien (1807–81), once a pupil of Chūsai though only two years younger, scion of a well-known medical family, and himself an accomplished scholar and doctor (particularly noted for his knowledge of herbs).

The Mori were hereditary retainers, again based in Edo, of the house of Abe, lords of Fukuyama. Though very talented, Kien was prone to be very frivolous. Like Chūsai he was a lover of the kabuki theater; but whereas Chūsai never allowed his "weakness" (which for an academic man it was, strictly speaking) to consume him, Kien did. When he was hardly more than a boy he could mimic his favorite actors with remarkable skill; and eventually he was as good as a professional.

For someone like Chūsai or Kien to be fond of the theater, so long as one did not become too obvious about it, was more or less acceptable. One talked about the theater with friends in the drawing room; one could visit it even, provided one did so quietly and not too frequently. And if Kien was known to go to the theater far too often, this was still something one could pretend not to know; and if he did occasionally flaunt his theatrical inclinations before others, one could regret it, but still hope that it was youthful enthusiasm. The trouble with him, however, was that he did not know when to stop.

It had been the custom of one of Chūsai's former teachers, the smallpox specialist Ikeda Keisui, to give a party for his students at the beginning of every year. In 1838, the year following his death, his son Zuichō gave such a party. But this turned out to be a more vulgar affair, with geishas in attendance and entertainment provided for the amusement of the guests. The entertainment included impressions of actors by Kien. Chūsai, at first silent, finally could not stand the vulgarity any longer and made known his disapproval. Zuichō, contrite, sent away the geishas. But clearly it had little effect on Kien, for soon afterward he was seen actually performing on the stage by a maid from Lord Abe's mansion. Highly amused and meaning no harm, she talked about it to others in the mansion; and when the story reached the ears of Lord Abe's senior retainers, it was decided that Kien had gone too far; he would have to be cashiered.

That these senior officials had known about and tolerated Kien's infatuation with the theater for some time cannot be doubted. But what they did not know was that he had in secret become a part-time professional actor and had been displaying himself before the common folk. Their indignation is perfectly understandable: how many well-placed academics or clergymen in America or England in the nineteenth century would have been forgiven for such antics? And so Kien became a rōnin, a disgraced former gentleman without office or stipend. His friends, including Chūsai, tried very hard to have him reinstated; but he had exhausted the patience of his domainal superiors, and their efforts on his behalf were in vain. Soon, destitute and deeply in debt, he fled from Edo one night, and became an itinerant doctor in the provinces, willing to practice any form of medicine—performing surgery (though by training an internist), setting bones, delivering babies, massaging stiff-muscled peasants, and even treating sick animals. He had with him his grandmother, mother, wife and child. The grandmother died during the ordeal, but the rest managed to survive. Finally he ended up in the town of Ōiso, about forty miles south of Edo, where a former pupil was a townsman of influence. Through this man's good offices Kien came to be accepted in the town as a doctor of renown from the great city.

'As his practice in Ōiso became more successful and his circumstances easier he took to visiting Edo occasionally. And the understanding was that when he did so he would stay in the Shibue house for about a week. There was nothing furtive about the way he would come to Edo, nothing to suggest that this was a man who had ignominiously fled the city by night. Tamotsu remembers his mother telling him that Kien would come dressed in a kimono of striped crepe silk and wearing a sword with a vermilion-lacquered scabbard carved in the style of a shrimp shell; and when he went out for a walk, he would hitch up the ends of his kimono so that his delicately tie-dyed loin cloth would show. [In other words, he dressed like a swaggering, déclassé fop.] His admiration for the famed kabuki actor Danjūrō VII was known to many; and if a passerby on the street called out to him, "Hey, Danjūrō!" he would stop and adopt the stylized stance of the actor coming to a sudden standstill. One notes that he was already approaching forty then. It should also be pointed out that his wearing a kimono of crepe silk was not necessarily an extravagance, since in those days a whole roll of the material [about twelve yards] apparently cost only a little over half a ryō. As Tamotsu remarked, anyone of ordinary means then could probably afford to wear it if one had a mind to.

'During the period when Kien would come to stay with them the Shibue had a maid named Roku. Io had had her as a personal maid when she was working in the Tōdō house, and had brought her with her when she married Chūsai. Kien took a fancy to her, and never seemed to tire of chasing her all round the house. One day he knocked down a great lantern while grappling with her. The floor mats were of course soaked with oil. Io in jest wrote a solemn poem of reproof, severing all ties with Kien, and had it taken to him. Actually, Kien was not the only guest who tormented Roku: Hōkaishi, too, was in the habit of chasing after her whenever he came to the house. Not long afterward she left, a suitable husband having been found for her with the assistance of the Shibue.

'Kien, being of the opinion that Chūsai's eldest son Tsuneyoshi, then barely twenty, was far too well-behaved, tried several times to take him to a brothel in Yoshiwara; but Tsuneyoshi would not listen. Kien then appealed to Io, thinking that her tacit permission, if conveyed by him to Tsuneyoshi, would change the young man's mind. The result was a series of arguments between Kien and Io. It was not that she herself necessarily disapproved; rather, what prevented her from giving even the slightest suggestion of tacit approval was her awareness that her husband looked upon anyone's going to Yoshiwara as a grave moral offense.

'Kien's visits to Edo, however, were not for recreational purposes. What he was hoping for was that his former lord, Abe Masahiro [1819–57], would take him back as a retainer; or, failing that, the Shogunate, in recognition of his abilities, would appoint him; and the chances of either happening would of course be increased if he were occasionally to come to Edo. The Shibue house, then, was his base of operations, so to speak, in his campaign for recall to the city.

'At a glance it might appear that of the two possibilities of employment Kien had in mind—appointment for the first time by the Shogunate and reappointment as a domainal retainer by his former master, Lord Abe—the latter would have been more feasible. But in fact the situation was quite the opposite; for in Lord Abe's eyes, the fact that Kien was a scholar of recognized ability, widely known especially for his knowledge of herbs, made his incorrigibly frivolous ways all the more reprehensible. [This Abe Masahiro became the Premier Councillor of the Shogunate at the age of twenty-six and died in office at the age of thirty-eight, having worked hard in his last years to save the Shogunate in the face of threats from abroad and within. He was no effete, self-indulgent aristocrat, and if anyone had the right to be angry with Kien, he did.] On the other hand, the Taki family [a medical family of the utmost importance in the Shogunate], in particular Taki Saitei [1795–1857; then senior personal physician to the Shogun, and brother of the head of Seijukan], were in accord with Chūsai, who maintained throughout that it was Kien's scholarship that mattered and not the frivolity of his private life. . . . And so it was to Taki Saitei that the Izawa brothers, Shinken and Hakken, and Chūsai appealed when their efforts to mollify Lord Abe had failed. Their proposal, which Saitei accepted, was that Kien should be given some kind of task under the sponsorship of the Shogunate, and then later, when he had regained some respectability, they could once more try changing Lord Abe's mind. Their strategy was entirely successful.'[2]

Kien was first promised an appointment as assistant in a major project then being undertaken by Seijukan—the preparation of an edition of *Senkinhō*, an ancient Chinese medical text;[3] then Lord Abe finally relented, and Kien's name was reentered in the domainal register. His reinstatement as Lord Abe's retainer took place in June of 1848; his appointment at Seijukan was made formal in September of the same year. He had left Edo in disgrace in 1837; his exile, then, lasted eleven years.

'Now Kien and his family could return to Edo. Before they arrived Chūsai found for them a house for rent near his own house in Otamagaike, paid the deposit and some rent in advance, and saw to it that it was supplied with the basic household utensils. As for clothes, it transpired that only Kien in the family had a decent wardrobe, the reason being that he at least had had to look respectable when as a general practitioner in the provinces he went on housecalls. The rest had no more than what they were wearing on arrival. "Why, she might as well be naked," said Io of Katsu, Kien's wife. She got together a whole outfit, including hair ornaments, socks, and clogs, and sent it to Katsu. For a while thereafter Katsu seemed to regard Io as a substitute family storehouse, and would come to pick up whatever item of clothing she happened to need at the time. Once, after Katsu had come and gone away with her most recent acquisition, Io remarked that that made it the sixth underskirt of white crepe. . . .'[4]

Undisciplined men were commonplace in Io's life, obviously. Confucian moral discipline was of course still the standard of her society, and presumably there were plenty of men like Chūsai who more or less lived up to it. But it would seem that as Edo culture reached its peak and was approaching its end, there was indulgence in the air as perhaps there never had been before; and the great urbanity that characterized much of Edo society at the time was perhaps inseparable from the abandon we see in some of Io's male friends and relations.

If Kien was bad, Io's stepson Yutaka was no better. Yutaka was Chūsai's second son, born to his third wife, Toku. Unlike the first son and heir, Tsuneyoshi, who, we remember, had refused Kien's offer of initiation into the ways of the world, Yutaka needed little encouragement in that regard. He was nine at the time of Io's marriage to Chūsai, and one may assume that for some years he was not the trial that he came to be. But by the time he was in his late adolescence, he was quite dissolute.

One of the best things that we know about Io, though not explicitly remarked on by Ōgai, is her relationship to her wayward stepson. She was extraordinarily loyal to him, and later, when she fell on hard times, Yutaka was equally loyal to her. About Tsu-neyoshi, the studious first son, we know relatively little. Born in 1827 to Sada, Chūsai's first wife, he was seventeen when Io married his father, and before he died at the age of twenty-seven, he was progressing nicely in his hereditary profession, and seemingly there was no reason to think that he would not have an honorable career as his father's successor. He was, one gathers, a quiet and decent person, and not half so interesting as his younger half-brother; for all Yutaka's wild and irresponsible ways, it is he who invites our sympathy, as he did Io's.

One of the more memorable passages in Ōgai's book concerns both Yutaka and Tō, Io's first and favorite daughter born in 1845. The time of the story is 1851, when there was an epidemic of smallpox in Edo. One of the families devastated by the epidemic was that of Yajima Genseki, a doctor retained by the Tsugaru and therefore a domainal colleague of Chūsai's.

'Genseki had no children by his first wife. His second wife Sumi . . . bore him two daughters. The older was named Kan, and the younger, Tetsu. On the twenty-fourth of February Sumi died; on the twenty-third of June Kan died; and on the fourteenth of July Genseki died. The sole survivor of the family was Tetsu, then only five years old.

'It was at this time that Yutaka became Genseki's "posthumous" adopted son, marrying Tetsu. The intermediary in this arrange-ment was one Nakamaru Shōan, a former student of Chūsai's.

'Nakamaru brought to bear all his persuasive power [he was good with words] to get Chūsai to agree to the arrangement. Principally he appealed to his teacher's compassion by saying that it would be unbearable to see the Yajima line come to an end. Such an appeal was necessary, for to give away his second son to the Yajima family was a considerable sacrifice for Chūsai; the girl Tetsu that Genseki had left behind had suffered a bad case of smallpox and her face was so disfigured that people would look away when they saw her.

'Moved by Nakamaru's words, Chūsai agreed to give his handsome son Yutaka to Tetsu. It was an arrangement that Io, out of sympathy for Yutaka, deplored. But because it was an expression of humane obligation on Chūsai's part, she could not very well make an issue of it.

'In that year Io lost two daughters: Tō, aged six, on the seventh of March, and Kishi, aged two, on the eighteenth. The other daughter, Kuga, aged four, had been put out to nurse at the home of one Shinhachi, a master carpenter in Koyanagi-chō. It was when Io, after the death of her two daughters, was thinking of having Kuga back that she had to receive Tetsu into her house and take care of her; and so Kuga remained with Shinhachi's family until the following year.

'Tō was a beautiful child. Of all Chūsai's daughters Ito [1831– 50; married in 1845, shortly after Io's marriage] and Tō were most admired for their appearance. Every time Io's elder brother Eijirō watched Tō dance he would say, "She makes me want to jump up and bite her." Io too made no secret of her admiration for Tō's beauty. Kuga once said to her, "The way you go on about how pretty Tō is, anyone would think I looked like a monster." And when Tō died, Kuga said, "You're sorry I didn't die in her place, aren't you?"

'For about six months after Tō's death Io's mind was unbalanced. Sometimes when the sun had set she would open the window by the garden and stare into the darkness, waiting for Tō to appear. Out of concern for Io's condition Chūsai finally had to admonish her, saying, "Io, you must pull yourself together. It's not like you to behave as you are doing."

'It was while Io was in this state that she had to receive Tetsu, the second daughter of Yajima Genseki, her stepson Yutaka's wife-to-be, and be loving foster mother to this child of strangers. She had to take the child to bed with her, and hold her as if she were her own. One night, in her sleep, Io thought the child in her arms was Tō; and then half-awake she began to stroke her gently. All of a sudden a certain fear assailed her, and she opened her eyes; and she saw Tetsu's face, the skin still red and taut, the pockmarks still fresh, right next to her own, almost touching. Losing control Io began to sob. Then when she had regained her calm she said, "Poor Yutaka."[5]

There is so much here that Ōgai leaves unsaid on purpose; and I must try not to be obvious where he is not. Yet I would like to say how typical a victim of the social obligations of those times Yutaka was, caught up as he was in circumstances absolutely beyond his control, forced to marry a young girl (the marriage would be consummated later, if it ever was) simply so that her family name might be continued. And what of Tetsu, the disfigured orphan girl placed in a house of strangers, destined to be the wife of a man who never wanted her? She later turns into a cold, nagging wife, and no wonder. Kuga, too, touches us. The irony is that she, of all Io's children, was most like her. Wilful and independent, unbroken by the memory of having been the less favored child, she develops a passion for nagauta singing at a very early age, and becomes a distinguished master of the art. She was still alive, we remember, when Ōgai wrote his book about her family, and still active in her profession.

Kuga's being put out to nurse was not such a heartless act on the part of her parents. It was a common enough custom then for the middle classes; and we learn later that when Kuga was born, Tō, then only two, was not yet weaned.

Yutaka, after becoming a Yajima, remained in the Shibue house for years afterward, and had eventually to be forced to set up his own house with Tetsu. The prospect of having to live alone with Tetsu could not have been attractive. Besides, he was a lonely person, I think (his mother Toku had died when he was nine, and there had not been much love between his father and mother), and he came to depend on his stepmother for whatever emotional support she was able to give. Unimaginably irresponsible, he was also an affectionate man, and not petty. When later his much younger half-brother, Io's youngest surviving child Tamotsu, was made Chūsai's heir after the untimely death of the initial heir, Tsuneyoshi, he showed no resentment. True, by the time of Tsuneyoshi's death he had already become a Yajima; moreover, he had by then become thoroughly disreputable, unfit to be anyone's heir. All the same, he had cause enough to be bitter about his lot; and it is impossible for us not to relate his unruliness to the lack of love between his mother and father, and to his enforced marriage to Tetsu as an "adopted" husband.

'Of the three children Chūsai had by Toku, his second son Yutaka was the only one still living. A libertine from youth, Yutaka caused his family considerable grief. A constant companion in his pleasure-seeking was one Shioda Ryōsan, a student of Izawa Ranken and son and heir of Shioda Yōan, who is said to have walked about balancing his walking stick on the tip of his finger. Ryōsan was the issue of Yōan and a young serving girl whom Yōan had seduced.

'I have already mentioned that Yutaka, not following the example of his father or elder brother, smoked tobacco. He was not fond of sake, however; and it might be said that both he and Ryōsan found their pleasure unaided by the intoxicant. . . .

'Once Yutaka appeared in the music hall under the name of Matsukawa Hichō [the characters for *hichō* meaning "flying butterfly"]. Ryōsan was put on the same bill under the name of Matsukawa Suichō [*suichō* meaning "drunken butterfly"]. Their specialty was the mimicry of known kabuki actors: preceded by loud musical fanfare each separately would appear on the stage and perform an excerpt from a kabuki play, imitating the voice and gestures of some actor. Yutaka's act came at the end of the bill [being the high point of the show]; Ryōsan's came earlier. When summer arrived the two would hire a large boat, and accompanied by musicians, would go up and down Sumida River enacting scenes from kabuki. One was the head of the Yajima family, hereditary doctors retained by the house of Tsugaru; the other was the young master and heir of the Shioda family, hereditary doctors retained by the house of Sō, lords of Tsushima. Indeed, Ryōsan's father had opened up a private practice in Kanda Matsue-chō, and had a city-wide reputation as a clever man and a good diagnostician. His fat face—so fat that he was often mistaken for a blind man—was familiar to a large number of Edo citizens. His was a most prosperous practice. Yet, despite the distinction of their families, these two young men felt no shame in exposing their faces on the music hall stage.

'That they drank little did not prevent them from visiting one restaurant after another in this and that quarter of town [where of course they would be attended by geishas and served quantities of sake], or from going frequently to brothels in Yoshiwara. And when they incurred debts at these various establishments, they would entreat their relations and friends to pay them; or when the debts accumulated to the point where no one would come to their aid, they would simply go into hiding. . . .'⁶

In time Chūsai, in utter despair, had a room of incarceration built upstairs, with bars on the windows and doorway, so that his son could be thrown into it whenever he wandered home. This was probably in 1855, when Yutaka was twenty. Ryōsan was then eighteen. In 1856 Yutaka was demoted from *omote isha*, or doctor of the outer chambers, to *kobushin isha*, or doctor of low status, a rank so low that as far as one knows, his father had never had to go through it. And because the Yajima were also Tsugaru retainers, Chūsai himself could not escape punishment by his lord, and was confined to his house for three days.

Yutaka must have mended his ways temporarily—he was to get into far worse trouble later—for in 1857 he was promoted to assistant doctor of the outer chambers, a step toward the recovery of his former position. But clearly Ryōsan did not.

'[In the same year] Ryōsan, who had been put in Asaka Gonsai's academy [Gonsai, 1791–1880, was a prominent Confucian scholar and teacher], one day pocketed one hundred ryō belonging to his mentor and fled to Nagasaki. His father Yōan, after paying Gonsai back the money, sent a man off to Kyūshū to fetch his wayward son. When Ryōsan was found he had not yet spent all the money he had absconded with; and so on his return journey with his father's man in tow, he spent what he had left with princely abandon at each of the post stations. It so happened that traveling at the same time was Hosokawa Nobugorō, fourth son of Hosokawa Narimori, lord of the Kumamoto domain, assessed at 540,000 koku. This young nobleman was on his way to marry a daughter of Lord Tsugaru Yukitsugu and become the adopted heir. His father, Hosokawa Narimori, wishing to expose him to the common people during the journey, commanded that he travel incognito. He and his retinue therefore were careful to avoid any show of extravagance, and remained inconspicuous throughout the journey. There were times when they and Ryōsan stayed at the same inn; and always it was Ryōsan, ignorant of the identity of Nobugorō, son of the lord of a domain assessed at 540,000 koku, who haughtily demanded and received attention. Nobugorō, who was only sixteen at the time, is the present Count Tsugaru.'7

It may surprise the reader to learn that in the previous year, the year of Yutaka's demotion and Chūsai's temporary confinement in his house, Ryōsan had been expelled from his house by his father, that the Shibue then had actually taken him into their house, and that it was Chūsai who had put him in Gonsai's academy. Chūsai's patience seems to have been nearly as inexhaustible as Ryōsan's capacity for mischief.

I would add that Chūsai's generosity in taking in students such as Ryōsan—and there were others—who were homeless but who in his opinion had talent, was in part due to his philosophical belief that the best way to influence the world for the better was to cultivate the best qualities of any given individual, and adopt a lenient attitude toward his or her defects. He found justification for his humane stance in the classics, especially in what has been translated as "the principle of reciprocity."8

It is something of a relief to know that both Yutaka and Ryōsan were good to Kuga, as was Chūsai, and that Kuga had fond memories of them. In his second reference to Kuga's early childhood much later in the book, Ōgai writes:

'In 1847 when Kuga was born, Chūsai's third daughter Tō was

only two and not yet weaned, and so Kuga was immediately put out to nurse at the home of one Shinhachi, a master carpenter living in Koyanagi-chō. When Tō died in 1851 at the age of six, Kuga, then four, was to be called back to her family, but her return had to be postponed because of the sudden entry into the Shibue household of the orphaned child Yajima Tetsu. When at last in the following year Kuga was allowed to return home, she was a lovely light-skinned girl of five. But because Io's heart was still full of sorrow over the loss of Tō, she could not give Kuga much love and attention, and Kuga for her part had to behave with considerable reserve toward her mother.

'Chūsai, on the other hand, loved Kuga, and kept her at his side and had her do things for him. Once he said to Io: "I'm a hardy fellow, and likely to outlive you. That's why I'm training her now to be your substitute when you're gone."

'Kuga's elder half-brother Yajima Yutaka and his friend Shioda Ryōsan were also among those who loved her. Whenever Kuga was practicing calligraphy and Ryōsan happened to be in the house, he would sit beside her, hold her hand and guide the brush. Once, when Kuga showed her father a finished specimen of her handwriting, he said teasingly, "Master Ryōsan writes rather well, doesn't he?"

'From the time she was little Kuga liked to sing nagauta, and on cold nights in the winter, when the air was sharp and clear, she would go to the top of the mound in the garden and exercise her voice.'[9]

Ōgai's sketch of Kuga is quite beautiful. It is clear that he was deeply attached to her; and though she does not appear much in the narrative, we come to know enough of her to realize what a truly impressive person she was.

Men like Yutaka and Mori Kien, for all their wildness, seem to have possessed a capacity for survival. Years afterward we see them functioning well enough, though not with what one might call distinction, as civil servants in the new Meiji government. Io's brother Eijirō and her brother-in-law Sōemon, on the other hand, while not quite as unruly as those two, were more inept. They both died before the Restoration, so neither had to face the challenge of surviving under the new regime. But one would guess that neither would have fared too well.

'Io's brother Eijirō had behaved himself for about three years after their father Chūbei's death; but then he reverted to his old habit of visiting Yoshiwara. He was about thirty at the time. The woman he went to sleep with was the same Hamateru that he had earlier found irresistible. In due course he put up the redemption fee for her and made her his wife; and in January of 1847, he retired from the headship of Hinoya, naming Io's daughter Tō, who was then barely one, his successor, and under the new name of Hirose Eijirō bought himself a seat on the gold exchange.

'Io's brother-in-law Nagao Sōemon drank constantly after succeeding to the family dealership in lacquerware. Showing no interest whatsoever in the business, he left its management entirely in the hands of his senior employees. His wife Yasu, being much too gentle by nature, made no attempt to remonstrate with him. Such passivity in her sister irritated Io whenever she visited them, but she could hardly interfere. Sōemon, oblivious to Io's irritation, welcomed her visits, and would detain her for hours talking about the personages described in *Shiji tsugan* [a monumental work of Chinese history completed in 1084][10] or other like subjects. And when she insisted on leaving, he would command his two young daughters, Kei and Sen, to prevent their aunt's departure. Crying, they would beg Io to stay. They cried because when she left, the house would again become silent and their father's ill-humor would return. Helplessly, Io would remain yet a little while longer. And once home, she would tell Chūsai what she had witnessed.

'Chusai became so concerned about the condition of Sōemon, who not only was Io's brother-in-law but had been at college together with her brother Eijirō, that one day he took it upon himself to call on him at his house in Yokoyama-chō and at length admonish him. Put to shame by the visitation, Sōemon began to show a little more interest in the family business.'[11]

While Sōemon seems capable of at least showing some signs of bestirring himself, Eijirō just fades away, resigned to his own lack of energy and to the conspicuous presence of it in his sister, presumably living in passive contentment with the former courtesan. Unlike Sōemon he was childless. He died in 1855, four years after the death of his niece and heir, Tō, of whom he was so fond.

For all his faults Sōemon was a livelier person. And whatever Io may have thought of him, he himself was very admiring of her.

'There is a story behind Sōemon's great trust in Io's judgment, a trust which went far beyond the respect he would have had for her as Chūsai's wife. It began when once Io severely admonished him for his tyrannical behavior toward his family, in particular his habitual mistreatment of his wife Yasu. The effect of Io's admonishment was such that Sōemon broke down in tears and begged to be forgiven. Ever since then, he held her in extremely high regard.

'Sōemon was a man without guile, honest to a fault. But he was quick-tempered. The incident I am about to relate took place in 1846. Sōemon had already begun to tutor his daughter Sen, who was then only six, saying, "She's going to be a samurai's wife." Sen was a quick learner, and read the texts assigned to her well. During the lessons, however, when Sōemon had drunk more than he should, he would playfully start hitting her on the head with his pipe, saying, "This is a lesson in fortitude." For the first few times that this happened Sen silently endured the ordeal. But one day finally she decided to resist, and crying, "Papa, don't!" raised her hand as if to strike back at Sōemon. "How dare you raise your hand against your father!" he shouted in a rage, and began hitting her in earnest. And when Yasu tried to intercede, Sōemon turned on her, and pulling her down to the floor by her hair, now began to beat *her*. "Leave the house at once!" he shouted.

'Theirs had actually been a love match [at least on his side]. It was on a certain day in April of 1834 that Yasu, then nineteen and still in service at the Abe mansion, was given leave to go to the Nakamura Theater and spend the night at home. Sōemon also happened to be at the theater, and when he saw Yasu he was enthralled. He followed her to her house when the theater let out, and found that it was none other than Hinoya of Kon'ya-chō, the home of his college friend Eijirō. Realizing that she was Eijirō's younger sister, he immediately sent an intermediary to Hinoya with a proposal of marriage.

'It was this very same Yasu, then, who fled in a disheveled state to her brother Eijirō's house to escape further beating by her husband. Eijirō at the time was still head of Hinoya, and preoccupied as he was with business matters, had no inclination to go to his brother-in-law and try to placate him. His wife Hamateru, the former courtesan, had turned rather feeble and was not the sort to turn to in a crisis. But Io happened to be visiting, and so Eijirō turned to her.

'After calming Yasu down she went back with her to her house. There she found Kei wandering about the house in a daze, and Sen still crying. Their father had helped himself to more sake after his wife's flight, and now greeted Io with a ghastly grin. Io began by apologizing quietly on her elder sister's behalf, but Sōemon would not listen; and as they talked he became more and more voluble until he seemed entirely carried away by his own eloquence. Soon he was citing recorded instances in China and Japan of women who had been divorced by their husbands, who had betrayed their husbands, and so on. Deciding that he would go on forever in this righteous and erudite vein if left unchallenged, she resorted to argument by authority also, citing examples from resounding Chinese sources of virtuous mothers and considerate husbands.[12] In the heated exchange that ensued Io was quite remorseless. And as Sōemon finally acknowledged defeat, he said: "Why weren't you born a man?"'[13]

Actually, in the original account that was given Ōgai, Sōemon is quoted as saying, "Why weren't you born with testicles?" It was one of Ōgai's burdens that he was writing in a less candid age.

In those days it was customary even for merchants of Sōemon's class to live and conduct their business in the same premises. In 1852, however, he decided to give over their house in Yokoyama-chō entirely to business and build a new family residence in Hon-chō 2-chōme. While this plan was being put into effect he, Yasu, their two daughters, a maid, and an apprentice stayed with the Shibue for two years, occupying four rooms upstairs. The Shibue house at times must have been like a small zoo.

One might say that such hospitality extended by the Shibue to Sōemon and Yasu was a matter of family obligation. But the fact is that Chūsai and Io were unusually kind, and there were several others besides Kien, Ryōsan, and living-in students (sometimes as many as ten) who were taken into their house when they had nowhere else to go.

A lay nun by the name of Myōryō-ni, born in 1781, was one of these. Ōgai writes:

'Myōryō-ni originally had no particular ties with the Shibue. She was born to a family that owned a second-hand clothes shop in Kanda Toshima-chō, and in her youth served as a page to Lady Shinju-in, widow of Lord Tsugaru Nobuyasu. This Lady Shinju-in was very fond of Chūsai when he was a little boy, and constantly had him at her side to watch him play. After leaving service Myōryō-ni got married; and when her husband died she took the vow. Her late husband's younger brother, who had once been in love with her and now hated her, began to mistreat her badly when he became the new head of the house. For some years she suffered the cruelty in silence. Unfortunately, when this man's son succeeded to the headship of the family, the cruelty toward her doubled. Then, to make matters worse, she caught eye disease. This was in 1845, when she was sixty-four.

'She went to Chūsai for treatment. Io, who had become Chū-sai's wife the year before, took pity on her when she heard about her misfortune, and offered her shelter in her house. There Myōryō-ni took care of Io's children, of whom she particularly loved Tō and Tamotsu.'[14]

This Myōryō-ni was to live with Io until 1868, when Io and her children were commanded to leave Edo for Hirosaki, their lord's domainal seat. Myōryō-ni was then eighty-seven, much too old to accompany Io to the northern castle town; and before they parted, Io made sure that Myōryō-ni would be well taken care of.

Another woman who came to live with them was Maki, the one who had incurred Io's hatred by referring to her mother as "that deafie." After Io's father Chūbei's death she had stayed on with Eijirō. But when Eijirō died in 1855, she became homeless, and either Yasu or Io had to take her in, for after all, she had been their father's mistress. There is no denying that in allowing her to come and live with her, Io showed a certain fortitude and dutifulness. But we have reason to believe that had it not been for Chūsai's coaxing, Io would not have tolerated Maki's presence in the house; and Ōgai is being slightly pompous when he praises Io for her act of generosity thus: "It was this same Maki, then, who in her old age came with her head lowered to receive the hospitality of the Shibue family. And so Io, in permitting this old woman to become a ward of her family, honored her mother's memory through charity, not revenge."[15] Anyway, the important thing is that whatever Io's attitude might have been, Maki was looked after until she died at the age of seventy-six in 1866, when Io herself had been a widow for eight years.

Then there was Toma, who was a half-sister of the late Toku, Chūsai's third wife. After Toku's death Chūsai had continued to associate with her father Okanishi Eigen, a doctor retained by Lord Abe, if only because Eigen was Yutaka's grandfather. Ōgai writes:

'Eigen was a simple and honest man; but he was disposed on occasion to indulge in behavior which went beyond the bounds of normality or propriety. Once he bought eight *mon*'s worth of cooked beans, put it away in a mouse-safe container, then went back to it at regular intervals to see if it had diminished at all. One day he dropped by at Chūsai's house on his way elsewhere, carrying a large mackerel. Presenting the fish to Chūsai he said he would drop by again on his way home. Io was now in a quandary as to what she should serve him with the sake when he returned, for on several occasions he had chided her for her culinary extravagance. "Serve him the mackerel he gave us," said Chūsai. When she duly did so upon Eigen's return, he ate with obvious lack of enthusiasm. At last he said, "We never serve such fancy food in our house." "But what you are eating is the mackerel you brought us," replied Io, but Eigen pretended not to hear. Presumably it was the way Io had prepared the fish that Eigen considered too fancy.

'What displeased Chūsai most about Eigen was his callous treatment of his daughter Toma, a bastard child borne him by a kitchen maid. In spite of the fact that he had formally recognized her as his child, he made her sleep on a single, unpadded straw mat laid out on a bare floor. "Can't have a dirty child like that sleeping on a padded floor," was his comment. His callousness was not made necessary by the presence of a resentful, scolding wife, for she was already dead by then; it was entirely attributable to his own perverse nature. Chūsai, with Io's concurrence, received Toma into his house, and later gave her away in marriage to a farmer in Shimōsa.'[16]

Apart from all such guests, varying in their lengths of stay, there were of course the Shibue children and servants. In 1852, say, when Sōemon, his family and servants occupied four rooms upstairs, there must have been about twenty-five people living in the house altogether, including Tsuneyoshi, Chūsai's eldest son, and his wife Ito; Chūsai's second son Yutaka, surnamed Yajima, and his "wife" Tetsu; Io's daughter Kuga; three or so menservants and as many maids; and several living-in students. In addition to all these people, there was Chūsai's enormous library, said at one time to have numbered 35,000 volumes. (These would be considerably slimmer than standard Western volumes. Also, by the time of Chūsai's death in 1858 the collection had been reduced to a fraction of its original size through pilfering and irresponsible "borrowing" by people like Yutaka and Kien.) No matter how spartan the living conditions of the students and servants might have been—and they cannot have been sordid—the house still must have been a large one by middle-class standards.

I am speaking here of the house of Honjo Daidokoro-chō that Chūsai and Io moved into in 1851. Their previous house in Otama-gaike in Kanda, where Chūsai was already living when Io married him, must have been smaller. Across the street from their house in Daidokoro-chō was the house of a *hatamoto* (bushi directly retained by the Shogun) named Tsuchiya Kuninao, titular Lord of Sado, who had a stipend of 4,000 koku. Although not a daimyo he was of near-baronial status, and the house and grounds of such a man would today provide ample space for a private school in Tokyo. The Shibue house would not have been so grand. But it cannot have been incongruous standing where it did, either.

It was in 1849 that Chūsai was presented to the Shogun, To-kugawa Ieyoshi (1793–1853). This was a rare honor accorded to very few doctors and scholars, and it carried with it the privilege of being entered in the Directory of Military Houses (bukan).[17] Ōgai notes that in the Directory for 1849 Chūsai's place of residence is not given; but that in the one for 1850 Io's own family residence, that is, the Yamanouchi residence in Kon'ya-chō, is listed as being Chūsai's. Ōgai suggests that probably Chūsai thought his own house in Otamagaike not quite grand enough for a man of his rank. (Presumably the move later to Daidokoro-chō was precipitated by such consideration.)

Ōgai tells a story in connection with the house in Otamagaike that illustrates what a mixed blessing the bestowal of honors could be to the recipient in those days:

'Custom required of those who had been received in audience by the Shogun to hold a great banquet. As for the appropriate number of guests to be invited to it, this too had been pretty well established by custom. Unhappily for the Shibue, their house had no room large enough for such an occasion, which meant that they had to add a whole new wing to it. But what would such an addition cost? Thirty ryō, thought Io's brother Eijirō, who then undertook to manage the project. Chūsai, aware of his own incompetence in all such practical matters, was happy with this arrangement; for was not Eijirō a businessman and a man of the world? But what Chūsai overlooked was that his brother-in-law, though born a merchant, was after all born a rather rich one, and had had far more practice at throwing money away than at making it or spending it wisely. Before the construction was less than half completed, then, they had spent well over a hundred ryō.

'For all his accustomed unconcern for money, Chūsai's face would now turn ashen every time he heard the sound of a saw or a hammer. His misery was such that finally Io, who had from the beginning entertained grave doubts about her brother's supervisory capacity in the venture, said to him: "You will think me very forward in saying this, but such a happy occasion as this happens rarely in a man's lifetime, and I won't stand aside in silence and watch it being spoiled by mere money worries any longer. Please let me take care of the expenses."

'Chūsai looked at his wife in astonishment. "But the expenses will come to some hundreds of ryō! Where will you be able to raise that sort of money? Are you sure you know what you are saying?"

'Io smiled and said: "I may be stupid, but not so stupid as to say what I said without some plan in mind."'[18]

The dialogue that ends the above passage is mostly Ōgai's invention, and it makes one slightly uneasy. It is not an instance of irresponsible dramatization, for according to the original account some such exchange did take place, but it is clumsily done. The rest of it is characteristically Ōgai, I think, a masterly retelling of family lore.

By selling clothes and pieces of luxurious bedding she had brought with her at the time of her marriage, Io raised three hundred ryō. This was enough to defray the cost of the addition to the house, but not the cost of obligatory entertainment and exchange of gifts; and so she sold her hair ornaments and the like to raise the rest.

If the Tsugaru authorities were not enthusiastic about Chūsai's appointment to the faculty of Seijukan, they were less so about his presentation to the Shogun five years later. Ōgai tells us that when Izawa Shinken, Chūsai's friend, the one who would come to chat with Io, was presented to the Shogun a little time before Chūsai, his master Lord Abe in recognition of the honor raised Shinken to an honorary rank nearly at the top of the domainal bushi hierarchy. Now, this may well have been connected with the fact that the Abe were "inside" (fudai) lords, while the Tsugaru were "outside" (tozama) lords. But whatever the reason, Lord Tsugaru's reluctant recognition of the honor bestowed on Chūsai by the Shogunate was almost comical in its meanness. Ōgai, never catty, cannot resist being mischievous when describing Lord Tsugaru's largesse: "Because of the general prestigiousness of the honor, it imposed on the recipient a considerable financial burden. Lord Tsugaru, mindful of this, presented Chūsai with a loan of three ryō, which he was to return within a year. Though appreciative of his lord's goodwill, Chūsai was at a loss to know what he should do with the money."[19] It really was rather like a great Scottish chieftain in mid-nineteenth-century London granting a clansman who had just been knighted by the English king a loan of, say, three pounds to mark the occasion.

Chūsai's stipend from the domain remained the same—that is, a little over three hundred koku. By the standards of domainal retainers, this was highly respectable. The family that Chūsai's second wife Ino came from, the Hirano, received about the same, and they were important bushi, being rusui, or liaison officers, of the domain. Socially, three hundred koku placed families like the Shibue and the Hirano in the middle ranks of the gentry. But as income, when the stipend expressed in rice amount was translated into money, it was a pittance compared to what a merchant like Io's father could command. According to Io's notes, her husband's domainal stipend came to five ryō and one *bu* (four bu made one ryō) a month.[20] This becomes hardly believable when we remember being told that it cost Io's father four hundred ryō a year to keep her in service at the Tōdō mansion. Of course, much of this very large sum would have been spent on fine clothes and gifts. Also, the monthly income from Chūsai's official stipend, as recorded by Io, presumably represented what was left after Chūsai had taken out of the domain's storehouse in Edo the actual rice that his household would consume. Yet if we reckon that Io's father had an annual income several times what it cost him to keep her in service, we have some idea of what a gap there was, economically speaking, between such domainal retainers as the Shibue and the Hirano, well-placed though they were, and some merchants. And Io's family were not of the truly rich of their class.[21]

Chūsai received an additional stipend from the Shogunate, but this came to hardly more than a nominal sum. Had Chūsai had to live on his official stipends, then, he could not have lived quite in the style that he did, any more than a cleric making less than a hundred pounds a year could have led an upper-middle-class life in London in the middle of the nineteenth century. But what made it possible for him to live as he did—not extravagantly but with some style—was the right granted his family in his father's time by Lord Tsugaru to manufacture and sell the medicine known as ichiryū kintan. This brought Chūsai an income, we are told, of over a hundred ryō a month[22]—an income which put him far above the middle-class bushi level financially.

There was also Io and her trousseau. In those days Japanese women did not have jewelry of precious stones, so that her valuable possessions would have consisted of exquisite silk kimonos, obis, and undergarments, and hair ornaments of lacquer, coral, tortoise-shell, and silver, all made by artisans of the first class. It is sometimes imagined that such things, prohibitively expensive today if at all available, were relatively cheap in those days. But this was not the case, and very few wives or daughters of bushi would have possessed even a fraction of what Io had.

We remember that for whatever reason, Io had yielded the right to inherit the family estate to her brother. But though Ōgai is silent on the subject, I would suspect that one way or another she had access to the family money, whether in the form of an allowance from Eijirō, or assistance when needed.

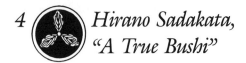

4 Hirano Sadakata, "A True Bushi"

Chūsai's brother-in-law Hirano Sadakata (he was not only the brother of Chūsai's second wife Ino, but Io's adoptive brother) was considerably more hard-pressed for money than Chūsai and Io were, partly because he did not marry as well, partly because he did not have Chūsai's source of additional income, and partly because his style of life was perforce more extravagant. Ōgai's description of the sort of man this Sadakata was, and of the way he lived, is the finest such sketch of an authentic bushi of the time that I know of.

'When it was decided that Io would marry Chūsai, she became the adopted daughter of Hirano Bunzō. Bunzō's son Sadakata, an officer of the Tsugaru domainal constabulary stationed in Edo, was the same age as Io's elder brother Eijirō, having been born in 1812. Io therefore became his younger sister. However, because Io was to wed a man to whom his late elder sister Ino had been married, he chose to address her as his elder sister.

'Bunzō's opinion was that if he was to act as Io's father in the coming marriage, there ought to be some semblance of a true father and daughter relationship between them; and so he took her into his house three months before the marriage and kept her close to him, having her fill his pipe, make his tea, and serve the sake.

'Sadakata was a soldierly, dashing sort of fellow who affected a

hairstyle favored by certain fashionable young men about town—
almost all of the hair shaved off with very thin strands of hair left
on the sides and then pulled back into a top-knot—and who
customarily wore a black pongee kimono imprinted with the family crest [a white insignia on each side on the front below the
shoulder, one on each sleeve, and one on the back just below the
collar]. He already had a wife, named Kana, née Aibara. The two
had been caught having a love affair before they were married and
had been disowned by their families. For a time they lived together in some shabby back street; but their parents, always fond
of them, had eventually relented and allowed them to get married
with their formal approval. . . .¹

'On the second of June, 1850, Hirano Bunzō died, and in his
place his son Sadakata was promoted to liaison officer. The promotion put Sadakata in the so-called lone salutation class within
the domainal hierarchy—that is, at a gathering of the Tsugaru
bushi before their lord, those of that class would go forward and
make their obeisance singly, followed by those of lesser rank who
would present themselves in twos, then threes, and so on; and
when finally it was the turn of the "horseless" retainers to make
their obeisance, they would do so en masse.

'The liaison officers of the various domains then stationed in
Edo formed what we might very well liken to the *corps diplomatique* in a modern capital city, and their style of life was notable
for its glitter and urbanity. In Sadakata, with his rakish hairstyle
and elegantly austere black kimono (he would not be seen in any
other form of dress), we see what must surely have been a quin-
tessential example of his breed.

'One hardly needs to be told, then, that he was not a bookish
man. Yet when we learn of his reverence for the classics and of
his desire to find in them guidance for his professional conduct,
we realize that he had a quality not shared by many of his professional colleagues.'²

Sadakata's "reverence for the classics" refers specifically to an
incident which took place on the day of his appointment as liaison

officer. On his return home from the Tsugaru mansion he sent a
brief note to Chūsai asking him to come to his house; and when
Chūsai arrived he asked him to give a lecture based on Confucius
on the responsibilities of a knight in serving his lord. Gladly
agreeing to do so, Chūsai gave a lecture beginning with the line
from the *Analects,* "Tzu Kung asked: 'What makes a man worthy
of being called a knight?'" And when the lecture had ended Sadakata turned toward the Buddhist family altar containing ancestral memorial tablets, and vowed to discharge his duties with
honor. According to Io, Chūsai was deeply moved by the experience, and said to her when he came home, "Sadakata is a true
bushi."

How nearly priestly, albeit in a secularized sense, was the role
of a Confucian scholar in Japan at the time, and how important
the spirit of reverence was thought to be in an ideal man of the
military, we can see from this incident. Yet behind the shared
reverence, the mutual respect, indeed their real fondness for each
other, there was finally the gap between the scholar-doctor and
the soldier. It was after his marriage to Sadakata's sister Ino that
Chūsai discovered to his horror that Ino's and Sadakata's late
grandfather, an accomplished swordsman and calligrapher, had in
the course of several nights gone out to the outskirts of Edo and
cut down one man after another to test his own skill. Chūsai had
then and there vowed to save as many lives as had been lost in
the rampage. We have no reason to believe that Sadakata had
inherited his grandfather's infatuation with the sword. But we do
know that later, disgusted with Yutaka's continued bad behavior,
he suggested that Yutaka be made to kill himself with the sword.
Chūsai was dead then, but he would never have thought of sug-
gesting such a recourse, not only for his own son but anyone
else's. Sadakata was a good friend to have—he was loyal to Io all
his life—but not the best person to annoy. And the fact of the
matter is that without the potential threat of the use of the sword,
no man could be a true bushi, not even in effete, nineteenth-
century Edo. Ōgai continues:

'Every morning after he had been appointed liaison officer Sadakata got up at sunrise. He would first go to the stable to see his beloved horse Hamakaze ["Shore Breeze"]. Once a friend asked him, "Tell me, why do you bother so much with that horse?" "Because," replied Sadakata, "a horse is ready to die with you." After seeing Hamakaze he would wash his face, rinse his mouth, then kneel before the family altar and say his morning prayer. His admonishment to the household was that while he prayed he was not to be disturbed on any account; if a visitor called, he was not to be announced until he had finished. When the prayer was over he would have his hair done. He would then have his breakfast brought in, which would always include a bottle of sake. That it was early in the morning made no difference; Sadakata had to have his sake. He was not particularly fastidious about the fish he got; but he was very fond of pressed fish cake made by Nodahei, the renowned fish-cake shop, and this he expected to see on the table without fail, whatever else was served. Nodahei's fish cake was a luxury, for at a time when a helping of eel casserole cost 200 mon and a bowl of buckwheat noodles topped with tempura 32 mon . . . , one slab of it cost 2 bu and 2 shu, or 3,755 mon. [There were 6,000 mon in a ryō. Sadakata, by the way, would not have eaten a whole slab in one sitting.]

'At ten o'clock, about the time Sadakata was finishing his breakfast, the great drum in Lord Tsugaru's upper mansion would sound. This was a particularly famous, or notorious drum which, according to city lore, had several generations before been deemed a public nuisance by the city magistrate, who prohibited the striking of it. [No wonder, for such drums were to be struck only when fire was sighted by certain authorized persons, of whom Lord Tsugaru clearly was not one.] But the Tsugaru family disregarded the prohibition, claiming that the striking of the drum was a family tradition. Instead, as a concession, they moved their main residence away from the center of Edo to east of the Sumida River. . . . At any rate, when the drum sounded the hour of ten, Sadakata would leave his house for his official quarters in the grounds of the Tsugaru upper mansion. After having taken care of business there, he would proceed to Edo Castle and meet his counterparts from the other domains. Accompanying him to the Castle would be his own retainers, a low-ranking samurai and a manservant, and other attendants assigned to him by his lord.

There were special "conference days" for the liaison officers, and on these days they would repair to designated meeting places after they had been to the Castle. They would meet at such famous restaurants at Yaozen, Hirasei, Kawachō, and Aoyagi, or at certain tea-houses in Yoshiwara, the pleasure quarter. At these meetings complicated, traditional rules of behavior were observed. To call these rules "etiquette" or "protocol" would be to lend them more dignity than they deserved; for they were like the custom of enforced drinking at male banquets, where one must drain the cup offered him, or like the rules of those German student societies. They were a serious matter for the members of this group, however, and sometimes mortal duels were fought because of them. Of particular importance was the custom of seating according to seniority: no senior liaison officer would move from his seat for a junior one, and the juniors were always expected to go up to the seniors and pay their respects as the meeting assembled.

The annual stipend of the liaison officer of the Tsugaru domain was fixed at three hundred koku, and in addition he was given a monthly expense allowance of eighteen ryō. . . . Remembering Io's note that Chūsai's stipend of three hundred koku came to five ryō and one bu a month, we may assume that Sadakata's combined official monthly income was something like twenty-three ryō and one bu. But his monthly social expenses ordinarily came to at least one hundred ryō. And there were frequent additional expenses. When there was a fire in Yoshiwara, for example, he was obliged to send a gift of a hundred ryō to Sanozuchi, an elegant brothel that he knew. Nor could he ignore the occasional request for a gift from his favorite courtesan Mayuzumi. Once, as the year approached its end, Sadakata said to

Io in private, "New Year's Day is at hand, and do you know, elder sister, that I haven't even the money to buy myself a new loincloth?"

'Sadakata had a colleague by the name of Hirai Tōdō . . . who, after having served as an officer of the domainal constabulary at the lower Tsugaru mansion, was then appointed liaison officer, shortly after Sadakata had been appointed to the same office. . . . Born in 1814, he was two years younger than Sadakata. . . .

'Sadakata was a strikingly handsome man, of a somewhat formidable, almost threatening, demeanor. Hirai, in contrast, was a gentle-seeming man; but he, too, was handsome, so that these two liaison officers of the Tsugaru domain were commonly referred to as the "twin Tsugaru stars."

'Serving under these two were, amongst others, Sugiuara Takichi, deputy liaison officer, and Fujita Tokutarō, clerk of the office. Sugiuara, who later changed his personal name to Kizaemon, was a man of sixty some years, fully versed in the affairs of the office. But Fujita, who changed his personal name to Hisomu after the Restoration, was then still a youth.

'One day Hirai ordered this Fujita to prepare a draft of an official document; and when Fujita duly presented the draft to Hirai, he was told by his scowling superior, "This won't do, Fujita. The style is pretty crude. And look at this handwriting! Go away and do it again." . . . It so happened that Hirai came of a family of accomplished calligraphers, and besides being one himself, could write poetry and prose of some merit. . . . Whereas Fujita had had no special training either in writing or in calligraphy. It could hardly be expected, then, that the revised draft he returned with would please Hirai. "Pretty bad," said Hirai as he handed back the draft to Fujita. "Is that the best you can do? If you can't do any better, you're not going to be of much use in this office."

'Fujita was desperate. As he thought of the disgrace to himself, the humiliation and the disappointment of his family, he could not hold back his tears.

'It was at this moment that Sadakata arrived. After listening to
Hirai's account of the situation, he asked Fujita to let him see the
draft he had written. "I can't say that I don't understand the gist
of what you've got here," he said, "but I can see why it wouldn't
satisfy Hirai. You've got to be a little more careful in the future."
He then picked up some writing paper, and wrote a version hardly
different from Fujita's draft. This he gave to Hirai, saying, "Do
you think this will do?"

'Hirai was obviously not impressed; but he could hardly criti-
cize the draft ostensibly composed by his senior. "Perfectly satis-
factory," he said, his manner now conciliatory. "I'm sorry to have
caused you all this trouble."

'Sadakata took back the draft from Hirai and gave it to Fujita.
"Go and make a fair copy of this. From now on, write your drafts
more or less in this way."

'Fujita merely said, "Yes, sir," and went away. But, we are told,
the gratitude he felt toward Sadakata was that of a man whose
very life had been saved. It would seem, then, that Hirai's ordinarily gentle demeanor hid an inner severity, while Sadakata, for-
bidding on the outside, had a more generous heart. . . .

'Both Sadakata and Hirai held in conjunction with the post of
liaison officer the post of company commander of domainal foot
soldiers in Edo. The rank of company commander, like that of
liaison officer, gave the holder the right to present himself singly
to the lord. When a fire broke out in the vicinity of the lower or
middle Tsugaru mansion, the company commanders, each dressed
in a fire-fighting uniform and mounted on a horse, would lead
tens of foot soldiers to the scene of the fire to protect the mansion.
On his way back to his office in the upper mansion Sadakata
would almost invariably stop by at the Shibue house. He is remembered on such occasions to have cut a particularly imposing
figure.

'Sadakata and Hirai apparently were both exceptional liaison
officers. Hoashi Banri [1778–1852; Confucian scholar and doctor]
once inveighed against the entire profession, saying that all the

domainal liaison officers, corrupt to the core, grew fat at the expense of the nation. And I daresay that many of the bushi appointed to this post made money out of it. But Io's son Tamotsu tells us that as a child, whenever he came across Hoashi's diatribe against Sadakata's profession, he could hardly restrain his anger, for he loved and admired the man.'³

Tamotsu's anger touches us; but it is also very difficult for us to understand exactly how Sadakata did make ends meet, if the figures we are given in the above account are right. We know that his colleague Hirai, who also was hard-pressed for money, pawned valuable heirlooms, which all such men of good family possessed. Perhaps Sadakata did the same. But going to the pawnshop can only have provided temporary relief. The most obvious explanation, then, is that Sadakata simply managed by not paying his bills, and getting heavily into debt, as so many fashionable bushi did in those days. One thing is certain, and that is that Sadakata did not make money out of his profession.

Sadakata and Chūsai had been friends from the time of Chūsai's marriage to Sadakata's sister Ino, but sadly they had a falling out a little over a year before Chūsai's death. The cause of it, in brief, was Chūsai's advocacy in 1856 of the proposal for partial withdrawal of the Tsugaru contingent from Edo. According to the proposal, the majority of the Tsugaru bushi in Edo, including the retired Lord Tsugaru Nobuyuki, would return to Hirosaki, the domainal seat in the far north, leaving behind Lord Tsugaru Yukitsugu and a minimal force of retainers. Proponents argued that the Shogunate, preoccupied as it was with diplomatic and internal problems—Commodore Perry had by then come to Japan twice—would do nothing to counter such a move; and it was time to heal the long-standing, bitter animosity between the Tsugaru bushi in Hirosaki and those based in Edo, and to have a unified domainal policy centered in Hirosaki. The proposal enraged Lord Tsugaru Nobuyuki and many others, including Sadakata, who, though Tsugaru bushi, were Edo men born and bred, and despised their country cousins in Hirosaki, whom they called "mountain apes." The proposal for partial withdrawal, then, with which Chūsai was identified, was defeated—at least for the time being; and amongst the prices Chūsai had to pay for his espousal of the unpopular cause was the loss of Sadakata's friendship.

For such a man as Sadakata, "returning" to his lord's castle town would have meant giving up all that Edo under the Shogunate stood for—its urbanity, enlightenment, its political sophistication—and having to live amongst provincial boors who spoke with guttural accents and hated everybody outside of their domain. In Hirosaki there were plenty of bushi with more distinguished lineages than his; but that didn't make them any less "ape-like" in his eyes. One can understand the way he felt. And what he could not forgive Chūsai for was his "betrayal" of what he, too, was born to.

5　Thieves and Earthquakes

Perhaps Chūsai could foresee more clearly than Sadakata the eventual fall of the Shogunate. The plan for Tsugaru's withdrawal from Edo which he had advocated was to be put into effect years after his death, only just prior to the fall. But until then, Sadakata's side seems to have held sway in domainal politics. Never entirely friendly toward the Shogunate, and traditionally connected with the kuge aristocracy in Kyoto through marriage, the Tsugaru were nevertheless slow to espouse the Imperial cause. But then, it was not that easy to declare for the Emperor when the Shōgun was still ensconced in Edo; and besides, the Tsugaru did emerge from the civil war unscathed (in so far as any daimyo did), unlike the more powerful Date family to the south of them, who steadfastly championed the losing cause. For their recalcitrance the Date were made mere modern counts by the new Meiji government, as were the Tsugaru, who were considerably lesser daimyo than the Date and for whom therefore the title was not an indignity.[1] The titular downgrading, of course, was simply a symbol of other, more serious disadvantages suffered by the Date and their retainers after the Restoration.

To what extent Chūsai's advocacy of Tsugaru's partial withdrawal from Edo was influenced by his pro-Imperial leanings is not clear. That he was indeed pro-Imperial, there seems little doubt, although there is no indication, as far as one can see, that he harbored marked ill will toward the Shogunate. This is not as contradictory as it may seem. For it was one thing to revere the Emperor on historical and scholarly grounds, and it was another to oppose, even covertly, a government that one had served. Chūsai was a moderate and conservative man, and I see not a hint of the revolutionary in him.[2] But however moderate and academic his Imperial sympathies may have been, they did once involve him in an incident which, as Ōgai says, nearly cost him his life. Ōgai cannot date the incident precisely, but he thinks it may have occurred in 1856.

'One day a man named Tejima Ryōsuke confided to Chūsai that a certain impoverished aristocrat [presumably a kuge nobleman of the Kyoto Imperial Court then residing in Edo] was in dire need of eight hundred ryō. Tejima was engaged in an effort to raise the money on behalf of the aristocrat, but he had little hope of success. Touched by Tejima's account of the aristocrat's predicament, Chūsai decided to raise the money himself and present it as a donation. And under the pretext of his own family's need he arranged for a loan of eight hundred ryō through a mutual loan association consisting of relations and old friends. The association duly assembled at his house and presented him with the money. That night, after these guests had departed, Io proceeded to have a late bath, for the very next morning she was to take the money to the aristocrat, who had already been forewarned through Tejima of her coming.

'It was while Io was in the bath that Chūsai heard visitors' voices at the gate. Then one of his menservants came to report that the visitors were three samurai, identifying themselves as messengers from the aristocrat. Chūsai agreed to receive them. As soon as the three men entered the room they asked Chūsai to send away the servants; their business was highly confidential, they said. Chūsai led them to a small inner room where privacy would be assured. There the three men informed Chūsai that the aristocrat had decided not to wait until the next morning for the money, and had sent them to get it that night.

'Chūsai declined to hand over the money to the visitors. The aristocrat had entrusted Tejima with the negotiations, he said, and the promise was that through no one but Tejima would the donation be presented; to accept three total strangers as intermediaries was out of the question. The visitors then explained why Tejima himself had not been able to come. Chūsai replied that he did not believe their story.

'The visitors exchanged glances, then stood up and holding the handles of their swords approached Chūsai. How dare he call them liars, they said; did he expect them to go back to the aristocrat like dogs with tails between their legs, their important mission unaccomplished? Was Chūsai going to give them the money or wasn't he?

'Chūsai remained seated for a while in silence. That they were impostors had been obvious for some time. But what was he to do? To engage them in swordplay was hardly the answer. There were menservants and students in the house. Should he call them or should he not, he wondered as he watched the three.

'It was then that the sliding door was pulled open. They had heard no sound of anyone coming down the corridor. In surprise Chūsai and the three men looked toward the doorway.

'Chūsai was sitting with his back to the wall, facing the three men. The door was to the side, and Chūsai, still facing the men, saw out of the corner of his eye his wife Io.

'She was an astounding sight to behold. Naked except for a loincloth tied around her waist, with a large dagger in its sheath clenched between her teeth, she was just bending down to pick up two wooden buckets she had put down on the corridor by the door. Steam was rising out of the buckets. They were filled with boiling hot water.

'Holding the buckets she walked in quickly and stood with her back toward her husband. She threw the buckets at the two men standing on either side of her, then drew the dagger out of its sheath. Glaring at the third man who stood in front of her with his back against the wall opposite Chūsai, she shouted, "Thief!"

'The two men who had been attacked with the buckets and the hot water were the first to run out to the corridor and from there into the garden. The third man rushed after them. Not one of them had thought to draw his sword, however threateningly he had continued to hold the handle.

'Io called the menservants and students by name, shouting "Thief!" after each call. But by the time they came, the three samurai had made good their escape.

'This incident became a favorite subject of conversation in the Shibue house for a long time after. But every time her exploit was described in her presence, she would leave the room in deep embarrassment. Ever since she had started serving in the great military houses as a girl she had always carried a dagger on her. This dagger, which was on the floor of the bathroom beside her clothes, she had picked up as she rushed out; but she had had no time to put on her clothes.

'The next morning Io took the money to the aristocrat's house. It could not be accepted as a gift, said Tejima; rather, it was to be a loan, to be repaid in yearly installments over a ten-year period. On several occasions later, however, Tejima was to come to the Shibue family to inform them that owing to his straitened circumstances, the aristocrat would not be able to meet his obligation that particular year. So that by the time of the Restoration, only a little part of the money had in fact been returned. . . .

'Tamotsu related this entire episode to me after much hesitation; and I, too, had doubts about committing the account to paper. But I could not bear to leave the world in ignorance of facts which so vividly affirmed Chūsai's good faith and Io's courage. Furthermore, the aristocrat is now dead. Perhaps, I thought, so long as I kept the aristocrat's role in the incident and his identity obscure, I could describe it without offense. Thus suppressing my doubts, I finally decided to give the above account in illustration of Chūsai's sympathy for the Imperial cause.'[3]

There are slight discrepancies between Tamotsu's original account of the incident and Ōgai's. One is that in the original version, Io appeared on the scene entirely naked. Another is that the menservants and students, four or five of them, armed with swords and sticks, did arrive before the ruffians fled from the room and caught one of them.

Whatever may be our preconceptions about the attitude toward women's nudity in Japan, the simple fact is that for a woman like Io, appearing before strangers and menservants—and indeed before her husband—without any clothes on was as shaming as it would have been for a similar Western woman, and it took courage and decisiveness. That even the mere mention of it embarrassed her deeply is an indication of the modesty of women of her background. And I see Ōgai's putting a loincloth around Io's waist as an act more of considerateness than of prudishness, as an attempt to lessen at least some of her embarrassment without departing too far from the truth.

As for the other discrepancy, I suppose it is an instance of Ōgai being in one of his more "creative" moods, although it is difficult to see how much less we would have thought of Io's courage had the third man not been caught. Perhaps it is connected with one important question which is left unanswered in the account: how did the three men know that there was eight hundred ryō in the house? It is, I suspect, part of the discretion that shrouds the entire account.

Chūsai seems not at all to have been bothered by his own passive role in the incident, and there is no reason why he should have been. But it must be said that selflessness in the face of physical danger was more in Io's line than his. In the great earthquake of 1855, we see Chūsai rushing out of the bedroom first without waiting for Io. Ōgai describes the scene without comment, and neither should we make much of it. But those of us with chivalric aspirations cannot but note it.

The earthquake occurred on the night of November 11. It had been cloudy that day, with rain falling intermittently. Chūsai had come back early from a theater party, and gone to bed after having a drink of sake.

'It began at about ten o'clock with two sudden big quakes; these then were followed by a steady rumble which gradually became more violent. Chūsai, lying in his quilted sleeping gown, jumped out of bed, picked up his two swords placed beside the pillow, and made for the front room. Between the bedroom and the front room was the lecture hall, where bookcases piled high stood against the length of one wall. As Chūsai was crossing the room these fell all about him, walling him in.

'Io too jumped out of bed and tried to follow her husband, but she fell even before she reached the lecture hall.

'In time their menservants came and helped them out. Chūsai's sleeping gown was torn from the hip down, but he had held on to his swords.

'Still in his night clothes Chūsai rushed to the lower domainal mansion in Yanagishima to inquire after the retired Lord Tsugaru Nobuyuki. From there he went to the upper mansion in Honjo. The lower mansion was destroyed by the earthquake, and Lord Nobuyuki later moved to the middle mansion. Lord Tsugaru Yukitsugu was at the time in Hirosaki, so that only his family were in the upper Tsugaru mansion in Edo.

'Chūsai met with Hirano Sadakata and discussed the matter of relief for the poor. Since his lord was in distant Hirosaki, Sadakata on his own authority—without even consulting Hirakawa Hanji, the head of the domainal treasury in Edo—ordered that 25,000 sacks of rice from the domainal storehouse be distributed to the needy citizens in the Honjo area. When later the Tsugaru bushi in Edo were ordered to return to Hirosaki, only one demurred, and that was this Hirakawa Hanji, who petitioned for an indefinite leave of absence, stayed on in Edo and opened a rice shop there in Fukagawa. [In other words, Sadakata was quite right in ignoring him, despite his high office, in time of crisis.]

'By the time Chūsai returned home all the houses in Daidokoro-chō had fallen down or were tilting badly. In his own house the room upstairs used for Yutaka's incarceration had been totally wrecked. [Luckily he was not in it at the time.] The house opposite, the one belonging to the hatamoto, Lord Tsuchiya Kuninao . . . , was on fire.

'That night the earthquake continued at intervals. The extent of the damage varied from street to street, but there was hardly a structure in the entire city that escaped damage entirely. The great statue of Buddha in Ueno lost its head; the nine-ring spire of the pagoda in Tennōji Temple in Yanaka fell, and that of the pagoda in Sensōji Temple was tilting. Fires started in scores of places, and it was only at about eight o'clock in the morning of the twelfth that they were finally extinguished. The number of deaths reported officially was four thousand, three hundred.[4]

'Tremors continued after the twelfth, and those whose houses had gardens pitched tents and stayed there, while many of the ordinary citizens slept out in the open. The Shogun Tokugawa Iesada took refuge on the night of the eleventh in the Takimi Tea Cottage in the Fukiage Garden within the grounds of the Castle; but since little damage was done to the main building of the Castle, he returned to it the next morning.

'The Shogunate established several relief stations to aid the needy—one outside the Saiwai Bridge gate, two in Ueno, one in Asakusa, and two in Fukagawa. [Food, tea, and money were provided at these stations.]'[5]

6 Chūsai's Death

If the Shibue and their relations survived that calamity without loss, they did not the next one, which was the great cholera epidemic of 1858. According to Ōgai this was the second such epidemic in Japan, the first having occurred in 1822.[1] It killed Chūsai and Io's brother-in-law Sōemon. It may or may not have killed the daughter born to Io that year, Saki, who died aged nearly two months on August 14, which was about the time the epidemic began. The cause of her death is not stated. Io was forty-two at the time, and Chūsai fifty-three.

'On the twenty-eighth of September Chūsai sat down to dinner as usual. But he would not have the sliced raw fish that was first served with the sake. "Why aren't you eating the fish?" Io asked. "My stomach is a little out of sorts," he replied. "I think I'll not have any tonight." On the next day, the twenty-ninth, which was a day when he was to be on duty at the middle Tsugaru mansion, he sent word that he would be absent on account of illness. That day he began vomiting. From then to the third of October his general condition steadily grew worse.

'Several doctors, including Taki Antaku, Taki Genkitsu, Izawa Hakken, and Yamada Chintei,[2] attended him, but their various efforts to cure him were in vain. . . .

'In delirium Chūsai would talk from time to time. To those

listening he seemed to be collating aloud passages from the *Ishinhō* [the tenth-century medical text he was editing at the time].[3]

'On the fourth there was a brief lull in his condition, which permitted him to state his last wishes. One of these concerned the education of Tamotsu, the designated heir. [We are not told precisely why Tamotsu, and not his older brother Osamu, was made the heir. One possible reason is that Osamu was not deemed bright enough, even though he could not have been more than three years old when that judgment was made by his parents; or, to put it a little differently, Tamotsu seemed brighter and more lovable even in his infancy. Another possibility is that Osamu was not a very healthy child. But whatever may have been the reason for Osamu's being passed over, the fact is that seniority did not give him the right to inherit the headship of the family, and in choosing Tamotsu as heir Chūsai and Io were not acting against custom.] Kaiho Gyoson was to teach him the Chinese classics; Kojima Seisai, calligraphy; Taki Antaku, the *Somon* [the ancient Chinese medical text].[4] Also, at some opportune time, Tamotsu was to learn Dutch.

'On the fifth of October, at two o'clock in the morning, Chūsai at last died. He was fifty-three. His remains were committed to Kannōji Temple in Yanaka.

'Surviving him were his widow Io, aged forty-two; his second son Yajima Yutaka, aged twenty-three, born to Toku, née Okanishi; his fourth daughter Kuga, aged eleven; his sixth daughter Miki, aged five; his fifth son Osamu, aged four; his sixth son Suizan, aged three; and his seventh son Tamotsu, aged one. Of these four sons and two daughters who survived him, all except Yajima Yutaka were children of Io, née Yamanouchi.

[Of all Chūsai's children, only seven lived to be adults; and of these, two died young—Tsuneyoshi, at the age of twenty-eight, and Ito, at the age of nineteen.]

'On the eleventh of April that year Yajima Yutaka had been restored by Lord Tsugaru to his original rank of physician of the outer chambers.

'Io's brother-in-law Nagao Sōemon had preceded Chūsai in death from the same disease a little over a month before, on August 28. And then in the big fire of December 19, the Nagao family lost both their residence in Yokoyama-chō and their business establishment in Honchō. These calamities led to the liquidation of the family business in lacquerware. Sōemon had left behind him his wife Yasu, aged forty-three, his elder daughter Kei, aged twenty, and his younger daughter Sen, aged eighteen. The three women were now homeless; and so Io had a small house built for them within the grounds of her own house in Daidokoro-chō, and received them there. Concerned about the continuation of the Nagao name, Io wanted Yasu to have Kei marry a man who would be adopted into the family; but Yasu was unable to bring herself to take any action.

'Immediately after Chūsai's death Hirano Sadakata tried to persuade Io to give up her house and move with her family into his. Because of a difference of opinion regarding domainal policy, he said to Io, he and Chūsai a year ago had temporarily become estranged from each other; but he had never forgotten their friendship, and had been hoping that soon he would once again enjoy a close relationship with Chūsai; but before his hope could be realized, Chūsai had died. He could never rest, he said, until he had repaid in some way his great debt of obligation to Chūsai. There were many spare rooms in his house. Would Io and her children therefore come and live with him, and regard his house as theirs? He was poor, true, but he had more than enough to cover day-to-day living expenses. He would never expect them to pay for their food and clothing. Living with him, they would be protected against the condescension of others toward a widow and her fatherless children; she would be able to save money, and with her mind at ease watch her children grow.

'In making such a proposal to Io, Hirano Sadakata showed he did not really know her. For Io was not a woman who would be content to be another's dependent. Of course she knew that with her husband dead, she would have to cut down her expenses. She would not be able to keep so many servants, or go on feeding all those semi-permanent "guests" who had collected in their house while Chūsai was alive. But there were hereditary menservants and aging women servants whom she could not bear to dismiss. And of the "guests," there were some who, if thrown out, would have nowhere to go. There were her sister and nieces, too, who would no doubt be rather helpless if forced to fend for themselves. How then could she, on whom so many others depended, suddenly become herself a dependent? Confident of her own powers, convinced that she was following the only course possible for her, she resolved to meet the challenge that faced her on her own. And so Sadakata's invitation was declined.'⁵

We do not see Io in mourning. This is not because Ōgai wishes to hide anything, nor because he wishes to present her in some conventionally stoical mold. Rather, it is because he does not wish to ask how she felt when her husband died. For him, the question is unnecessary. Some pages after the above passage, he tells us that Chūsai, while still in good health, had given Io a posthumous Buddhist name, and that in it he referred in anticipation to her place of death as Honjo, which was the area of Edo where they lived. "But," Ōgai adds, "changes that occur with the passing of time are beyond one's capacity to foresee, and Io was not permitted to die there."⁶ This is as far as he goes in expressing the sadness of Io's plight. Not surprisingly, his eulogy of Chūsai is also very understated.

'Though sympathetic to the Imperial cause, Chūsai was not anti-foreign. True, he at first disliked the West and was inclined to listen to exclusionist views; but he was made to reconsider his own attitude as he read Asaka Gonsai's writings;⁷ and as he proceeded to read Western works of natural history and philosophy in translations in classical Chinese, he was increasingly persuaded that Western learning was not to be lightly dismissed. So much so, in fact, that on his deathbed he expressed the wish that his heir Tamotsu should be taught Dutch, Dutch being then the principal medium of access to Western learning.

'A practitioner of Chinese medicine, he died just after the Shogunate had officially recognized "Dutch" medicine. The recognition came only after a bitter struggle on all fronts on the part of the "Dutch" school, and those who bore the brunt of their aggression were the practitioners of Chinese medicine. In such polemical works as *Kanran shuwa* and *Isseki iwa* we see how the latter in turn tried to discredit their antagonists.[8] Chūsai did not take part in the acrimonious debate, but we can imagine what sadness and grave uncertainty it must have caused him.

'I said that Chūsai died just after the Shogunate had recognized "Dutch" medicine. This recognition occurred in August of 1858. Chūsai died in early October of that year. . . .

[Not long before his death, it had been intimated to Chūsai that he would be asked to accept appointment as a physician of the inner chambers (*okuishi*) to the Shogun. His intention, confided to Io, was that if asked, he would go into retirement, in order to avoid the embarrassment of having to resign his domainal post. For unlike his appointment to the faculty of Seijukan, an appointment as okuishi to the Shogun would have necessitated his becoming a full retainer of the Shogunate.]

'But had Chūsai not died when he did and had he accepted the appointment with the Shogunate, he would presumably have had to serve with those doctors of the "Dutch" school who were appointed okuishi after its recognition. In which circumstance perhaps Chūsai, as a representative of the traditional school, might have had to involve himself in unpleasant and pointless disputes with his colleagues of the "Dutch" school, whose mission it was to introduce modern ways; or perhaps, unlike the authors of such works as *Kanran shuwa* and *Isseki iwa,* he might have helped pave the way for a more responsible comparative study of the two schools of medicine.

'Certain of Chūsai's daily habits which differed from the ordinary, I have already had occasion to describe. I would like here to describe a few more. A firm believer in preventative medicine, he adhered to a strict daily diet. At breakfast and at lunch, he would have three bowls of rice; and at dinner, two and a half. The size of the bowl was strictly regulated. In his later years Chūsai used only the bowl that Lord Tsugaru Nobuyuki had had made for him by Nagao Sōemon and given him as a present in 1849. It was somewhat larger than the standard size. Saying that a maid could not be trusted to fill his bowl with just the right amount always, Chūsai had his rice put in a small tub and had Io fill his bowl from it at the table. As for his miso soup at breakfast, he would have two bowls, no more nor less.

'His favorite vegetable was the large Japanese radish. When he ate it raw, he would have it grated; and when he had it cooked, he would have it done in the *furofuki* manner [boiled and covered with miso while still hot]. The juice from the grated raw radish, he would not have thrown away; nor would he have any soya sauce put on the radish.

'He had a constant supply of a special kind of fermented soybeans, prepared in a place called Hamana, some distance away from Edo, kept for him, and these he ate regularly.

'As for fish, he was particularly fond of bream pickled in miso and pressed, dried sardine. Occasionally, he would eat eel.

'He almost never indulged in eating between the main meals. Very rarely, he would eat gluten candy and the better sort of crackers.

'He never touched sake until he was thirty-two, when to ward off the cold in the northern castle town of Hirosaki, where he had accompanied Lord Tsugaru Nobuyuki, he began drinking. For a time, indeed, he drank rather heavily at dinner. But in 1854, when he reached the age of forty-nine, he decided not to exceed three cupfuls. His cup, by the way, was one that Io's father Yamanouchi Chūbei had given him, and this he would take with him whenever he went to a party.

'Before the earthquake of 1855, Chūsai never drank cold sake. But at the time of the earthquake he had occasion to taste it, and since then he would sometimes drink it, though never more than three cupfuls at any one sitting.

'Being fond of eel, he would occasionally have what was called "eel sake." The recipe for this drink was as follows: one put a piece of broiled eel in a bowl and poured a small amount of the drippings over it; then one filled the bowl with hot sake, placed the lid over the bowl, and let the contents stand for a while before drinking it. Since Io was not averse to sake, Chūsai after their marriage recommended this drink to her. Finding it much to her liking, she in turn recommended it to her brother Eijirō, her brother-in-law Nagao Sōemon, and Hirano Sadakata. These men were all won over by it.'9

Perhaps as part of what I have called a eulogy, much of the above may seem a little eccentric. But it is Ōgai's way of expressing his sense of the humanity of this man of the past whom, no matter how uncertainly, he has come to know. And it is characteristic of Ōgai that he should end his list of Chūsai's eating and drinking habits with Io passing on the recipe for eel sake to her three male relations. Through the mention of this trivial matter he reminds us of Io's loss, and makes us remember that of the four men she was closest to in her maturity, only one—Sadakata—still lived.

Ōgai then continues to describe other personal traits of Chūsai's which have come to his attention. Some of these we already know, such as that he loved the kabuki theater, collecting old directories of military houses, coins and maps, watching daimyo processions, reading popular fiction. He was deeply attached to his scholarly work, too, which consisted essentially of knowing the Chinese classics and the ancient medical texts.

What we did not know before is that after he had been presented to the Shogun a certain authority told him he would now be well-advised to stay away from the kabuki theater and public bathhouses. The latter injunction was easily enough followed, Ōgai tells us, since he had a bathroom of his own; but not to go to the theater was a heavy sacrifice. The theater party that he attended on the day of the earthquake was apparently his first visit to the theater in seven years. Another passion of his was gardening, and he did the pruning himself. His favorite tree was the tamarisk, which his father Tadashige also had loved. The one that Chūsai had in his garden when he lived in Otamagaike had been planted by his father, and it went with him when he moved to Daidokoro-chō, where it was replanted outside his study. He also loved to watch tumblers, and whenever an itinerant troupe came to the front gate to perform, he would rush out. What he hated most in his later years was thunder and lightning. Ōgai writes:

'This was presumably because he twice witnessed a lightning strike. One day, just after they were married, Chūsai and Io were walking along a street. The dark sky suddenly split above their heads, and a flash of lightning struck the ground right before them. There was a deafening noise, and they were both knocked down. The other time was when Chūsai was resting in the faculty common room at Seijukan, and lightning struck the garden in front of the lavatory near the common room. Izawa Hakken was in the lavatory urinating at the time. He fell forward when the lightning struck, hit his face on the urinal, and broke two of his front teeth. The two incidents, no doubt, were the cause of Chūsai's detestation of thunder. Thereafter, whenever he heard its rumbling, he would have his mosquito net hung, sit inside it, and have sake brought to him.'[10]

This particular phobia of Chūsai's, Ōgai notes, was shared by Mori Kien, the distinguished herbalist and would-be kabuki actor, who also lived in mortal dread of slugs. Even in total darkness, he would sense the presence of one of these creatures if it happened to be crawling across the street in front of him, and order his attendant to shine the lantern on it. To the attendant's amazement, Kien would be proved right.

The inconsequentiality of the way Ōgai ends his account of Chūsai's life is no less true or affecting than the solemnity of his tone as he informs us that he cannot stop here:

'Usually, a biography ends with the death of the subject. But in honoring a man of the past, one cannot but ask what became of those whom he left behind. And so, having finished recording the life of Chūsai, I am still unable to put down my pen. It is my wish, then, to continue this narrative and to describe the fate after Chūsai's death of his offspring, his wife and relations, his colleagues and friends.

'I am aware that when I do so, I shall find it impossible not to give offense to those still living, for my narrative, as it takes its course through time, must increasingly refer to them. In describing Chūsai's last years I have already had cause to hesitate for fear of giving offense. From here on, such causes for hesitation will become more and more of a hindrance to me. But I have resolved to put down in writing what I think I must, however difficult I may find it to do so. Then my work will be done.'[11]

I respect Ōgai's piety. But I do not think I do him an injustice if I say that had it not been for Io, his concern for Chūsai's posterity would have been less heartfelt.

7 *Incidents of Widowhood*

Io stayed in the house in Daidokoro-chō until 1860. This would suggest that although after Chūsai's death she had to trim her expenses, she was by no means in desperate straits. Besides, the house that she moved to—it was in Honjo Kamezawa-chō , and therefore not far from Daidokoro-chō—seems to have been a pretty large one. It had been a villa of the collector of boat tolls on Yodo River in Kyoto, and so presumably a fairly affluent man. The house had a sizable garden, with a pond large enough, we are told, to swim in. In the garden were also two small shrines, one of which was dedicated to the Fox Deity (Inari), and known locally as the Kamezawa Inari. On the day of the Inari Festival it was the custom for the people living in the neighborhood to come and worship at the shrine, and for twenty or so vendors to set up their stalls outside the gate of the house. When selling the house to Io, the owner set one condition, which was that she would permit the local tradition to continue. From such information we may infer that she still had the means to be a person of some consequence in the neighborhood.

With Io in her new house in Kamezawa-chō were her five children (the oldest of whom, Kuga, was thirteen, and the youngest, Tamotsu, three), the lay nun Myōryō-ni, Chūbei's old mistress Maki, Io's sister Yasu and her two daughters, and several servants (how many, we don't know). In one sense or another they were

all dependent on Io. It could not possibly have been an easier
time for her than Sadakata in his kindness had warned her it
would be, yet until the breakdown in 1868 of the way of life she
knew, the Shibue house remained intact, and retained its dignity.
She kept the household accounts, managed the servants, saw to
it that the house and grounds were properly maintained, looked
after two old women, supervised the meals, and then, on top of
all this (which one can argue is the lot of any mistress of a large
household), she supervised her children's studies in calligraphy
and the classics from noon until sundown, and made and dis-
pensed the patent medicine for which Chūsai had left her the
formula.

Yasu and her two daughters did not remain long in Kamezawa-
chō. Kei, the older daughter, was particularly eager to leave her
mother (we remember that Yasu had done nothing about adopt-
ing a husband for her so that the family business might continue),
and deciding on her own initiative to marry "out," got someone
to act as intermediary and left the choice of husband entirely in
his hands. A man was quickly found for her. This was one Rikizō,
owner of a tea house affiliated with a theater. Then her younger
sister Sen also got married, in her case to a cloth merchant.

Ironically, Kei's new husband was much impressed by his
mother-in-law's accounting ability, and took her in and put her
behind the accounts desk at the tea house. Yasu's future was thus
settled. What Kei thought of the arrangement, we are not told,
but presumably she approved. Perhaps some of the tension that
had come to exist between mother and daughter had been due to
the discomfort of living in the small house Io had had built for
them in Daidokoro-chō—it was small enough to have been
moved whole from there to the grounds of Io's new house in
Kamezawa-chō—and Kei's sense of the indignity of their dependence on Io.

After their departure from Kamezawa-chō, Yasu and her two
daughters more or less fade out of Io's life. Io cannot have admired
her meek and indecisive elder sister, who in effect allowed the

Nagao line to die out; and it is likely that she welcomed their departure. But characteristically she was always protective of Yasu, and we infer from Tamotsu's notes that when years later, during one of her absences from Tokyo (Edo had been renamed by then), she received news of Yasu's death, she felt the loss deeply.

Yajima Yutaka, the only adult male left in the Shibue household after Chūsai's death, had continued to live with Io in Daidokoro-chō. But when she moved to Kamezawa-chō, he at last separated from her. Two years previously, a few months before Chūsai died, he had been restored to his original rank of physician of the outer chambers. And then later in the same year, he was given permission to enter Lord Tsugaru Nobuyuki's inner chambers, though still holding the same rank. It was on the basis of such official recognition of his supposed reformation that Nakamaru Shōan, the eloquent former pupil of Chūsai's who had successfully advocated the adoption of Yutaka into the Yajima family, now argued that it was time Yutaka separated from Io and set up his own house with his wife Tetsu.

'Since there already were two or three others who expressed similar views, Io, though somewhat dubious, allowed herself to be persuaded. Seeing this, Hirano Sadakata, who at first openly disagreed with Shōan, became silent about the matter.

'The house in Honjo Midori-chō that Yutaka moved into had formerly been the residence of a certain town doctor named Sakuma, known to many by the nickname of "Pigeon Doctor." [Was he fond of pigeons, or did he look like one? Ōgai does not tell us.] Yutaka was joined there by his wife Tetsu, and with the one maid they hired, theirs was a small household of three. . . . At this time, Tetsu was already fourteen. Being a worldly man, Yutaka treated her as a child, gently and with understanding, so that there was no difficulty between them.

'However, now that he had moved away from Io's direct supervision, his life outside the house once more became unruly. No doubt he and Shioda Ryōsan had kept in touch after the latter's return to Edo from Nagasaki. Now these men did not merely frequent drinking houses and brothels: they went to gambling dens, where they played with men of criminal inclinations. It is said that Ryōsan in those days would walk the streets with his hair loose at the sides and the top of his head shaved, wearing a loose quilted gown in the manner of a professional gambler. Nemesis [Ōgai's own choice of word] was drawing ever closer in pursuit of Yutaka. . . .

'When the Shibue family moved to Kamezawa-chō, they discovered upon examination that Chūsai's library, once said to have contained 35,000 volumes, now contained less than 10,000. Once, in Daidokoro-chō, when Tsuneyoshi was still alive, he caught his younger brother Yajima Yutaka bringing books out of the storehouse, and immediately took them away from him. But there is no telling how many books Yutaka stole and sold without anyone in the family knowing. . . . From 1856 on Chūsai would often not feel well and lie in bed; and at these times books were apt to disappear. But his books were lost not only through outright theft; for many of the books he lent to friends and acquaintances—especially Mori Kien and his son Yōshin—were never returned. When Tamotsu started studying at Kaiho Gyoson's academy [in 1860], Gyoson's son Chikkei would occasionally warn the Shibue family that books with Chūsai's seal on them were being seen all over the city. . . .

'Sometime early in 1861, the third year after Chūsai's death, Io had three large boxes of books taken to Tamotsu's room and put in a shelved cabinet, and then said to him: "There are only three such copies of *Jūsankei chūso* [an edition of the Thirteen Classics] in Japan. See how good the printing is. Your father said they were to be yours, and since this year will be the third anniversary of his death, I thought it was time they were put beside you."

'Some days later Yutaka asked if he and his flower-arranging friends might have a party in Tamotsu's room. There was no room large enough for such a party in his own house, he said. Tamotsu duly removed himself for the occasion.

'After regaling themselves with sweet bean soup and the like

Yutaka and his so-called friends departed. When Tamotsu went back to his room and looked into the cabinet, all the books were gone.

'On the fifteenth of April of that year Yutaka, because of his disorderly conduct, was commanded to resign from his post and headship of the Yajima family and go into retirement. Lord Tsugaru, however, was pleased to permit the continuation of the family through adoption of a male heir.

'It was Nakamaru Shōan who undertook the role of intermediary in the hurried search for Yutaka's successor. Now, there was one Uehara Gen'ei, an associate physician to the lord with a stipend of 150 koku, who had come to be looked upon with favor by Nakamaru Shōan; and this man recommended a certain town doctor named Date Shūtei.

'On the eighth of September of that year, then, Shūtei adopted the Yajima name, and was given the family stipend of two hundred koku.' Yutaka, the adoptive father, was at the time twenty-six years old; and Shūtei, the adopted son, born in 1817, was forty-four. . . .

'Earlier, when Yutaka was given notice of his dismissal, the person most saddened was Io, and the person most angered was Hirano Sadakata. Sadakata severely reprimanded Yutaka, and asked him how he intended to regain his honor. Yutaka's answer was that he would like to enter Yamada Chintei's academy and continue his studies.

'Sadakata's condition for approval of the plan was that Yutaka must first show clear evidence of sincere repentance. So Yutaka and Tetsu moved into Sadakata's house, where they were given rooms upstairs.

'When November came Sadakata called Io to his house, and together they took Yutaka to Yamada's academy, which was in Hongō Yumichō.

'The monthly fee at this academy was three bu and two shu. A trifling sum, Sadakata said, but it ought to be paid by Shūtei, who was now receiving the stipend attached to the Yajima family; moreover, Shūtei should take Tetsu into his house and take care of her while Yutaka went to the academy. Shūtei was not pleased when Sadakata presented him with these two propositions. Indeed he was extremely ungracious at first; but in time, though grudgingly, he agreed to both.

'One suspects that when Uehara approached Shūtei about the possibility of assuming the Yajima name, he was actually acting as a broker, and that both men regarded the arrangement as a business transaction. Anyway, Uehara was a man who had little sympathy for the Shibue family, and was apparently in the habit of referring to Yutaka as "fart dregs."

'There were nineteen boarders in Yamada's academy. Not long after Yutaka entered there, he and a man called Umebayashi Matsuya were made prefects. . . .

'The appointment as prefect seemed to give Yutaka a measure of self-respect. He soon came to be trusted by families who needed medical care, and there were even hatamoto families who specifically asked for him. Seeing this, both Io and Hirano Sadakata were much relieved.'[2]

They were not to enjoy their sense of relief for very long, however. Early in the following year (1862), on the day of the Inari festival, Io held a party in honor of the Kamezawa Inari, to which relations and old friends were invited. During it Yutaka entertained all those present with a ballad-drama recitation and comic improvisations. Io was made uncomfortable by the performance, but thought that since Yutaka did not drink, little harm would come of it. When the party ended that night Yutaka departed with the rest of the guests. A couple of days later Yamada Chintei came to Io's house to ask if Yutaka was still there. He had not come back to the academy, Yamada said, since the day of the festival. Immediately Io sent out a search party, and Yutaka was quickly found. With not a penny on him he had gone straight from Io's house to a brothel in Yoshiwara, and was now lying low in a tea house in the quarter. After paying the bill Io sent him back to the academy.

A meeting was held in Io's house, at which were present Io;

Sadakata; Ono Fukoku, scholar-doctor and distant relation;³ and Io's son Tamotsu, who, though barely five at the time, was head of the Shibue house.

Sadakata was enraged. There was only one decent thing Yutaka could do, he said. He was to come to his house, and there, in the presence of those now at the meeting, commit *seppuku*. (Sadakata would not have used the more vulgar word *harakiri*.)

There is some question as to whether Sadakata truly meant what he said. At any rate, later, in a more moderate frame of mind, he was persuaded to agree to Io's counterproposal, which was that Yutaka should offer a written pledge of future good conduct to the Konpira Shrine in Tora-no-mon. The incident, then, ended rather anticlimactically.

To what extent Yutaka was chastened by this experience, it is hard to say. But Sadakata was a real threat, not a man to be trifled with; and it would seem that Yutaka, even if not completely re-formed, became less blatantly delinquent. We hear no more about him until 1867, when, at the urging of a friend who spoke en-couragingly of a doctor's prospects in Kawaguchi (a town north of Edo), he decided to go there, leaving Tetsu behind, and start up a practice. He did not stay there long, however; he was soon back in Edo, living, one is not surprised to be told, in Io's house. His comment to Io upon his return was: "All those cloddish country women—they won't leave a fellow alone. The country is no place for a single man, I can tell you."⁴

The fact that Yutaka was a charming and affectionate man can-not alone have compensated for all his less attractive traits in Io's eyes. But it seems that Io had a weakness for stylish men with looks and charm (though not of the surreptitious hand-holding variety), and they seem to have liked her. There was a bond be-tween her and such men as Sadakata and Yutaka, however ap-palling the two men might have found each other—a bond based on a shared dislike of the ordinary. Whether there were incestuous feelings between the two men and Io, I cannot say. Certainly Io in her forties was a vigorous woman (her last child by Chūsai was born when she was forty-two, in the year that Chūsai died), very confident, one can tell, of herself as a woman.

The account given below of Sadakata's second marriage, perhaps a little cruel in the telling, suggests the bond that existed between him and Io. In all essentials Ōgai's version is faithful to what Io's son Tamotsu gave him, except for a little dramatic license in the dialogue and description of gestures, and the modifying of Io's anger.

Sadakata and his wife Kana were childless. In 1861, when he was forty-nine, they adopted a younger son, then ten years old, of another bushi family of the Tsugaru domain. The boy's name was Fusanosuke. Although Ōgai does not tell us this—for fear, it is suggested, of offending Fusanosuke, who was still living in 1916—Io apparently objected to the choice, saying that the boy wasn't bright enough to be Sadakata's heir.[5] And then in 1865, at the age of forty-eight, Kana died. Ōgai writes:

'It was Kana who had made it possible for Sadakata to maintain frugality at home so that he might conduct himself with dignity outside as a liaison officer. After her death relations and colleagues repeatedly pressed him to remarry, but he resisted the pressure, saying, "I'm over fifty and I have no desire to be a bridegroom again." . . . For some time, then, he lived as a widower with Fusanosuke. But he began to listen to those who argued that a liaison officer could not perform his duties properly without a wife; and when, in 1866, a go-between recommended the daughter of one of the stewards of the outer chambers at Edo Castle named Ōsu, he was willing to consider the proposed match. The woman's name was Teru. . . .

'Sadakata instructed a subordinate of his at the liaison office in the Tsugaru mansion to call on the Ōsu family and see what Teru was like. The subordinate, Sugiura Kizaemon, was an experienced and reliable man whose judgment Sadakata trusted. Sugiura did as instructed, and returned to Sadakata with an enthusiastic report: Teru was not only beautiful but exceptionally graceful in manner and speech.

'Betrothal gifts were exchanged. On the day of the wedding ceremony Io went to Sadakata's house to receive the bride. She and Sadakata were sitting by the front window when the bride's palanquin was carried through the front gate and lowered in front of the house. Io could not believe her eyes when she saw the woman that came out of the palanquin. She was exceedingly small, dark-skinned, and flat-nosed. What was more, she had buck teeth which her pointed mouth could not conceal. Io turned to look at Sadakata. He smiled ruefully and said, "Well, elder sister, that I think is the bride."

'Some time passed between the arrival of the bride and the exchange of nuptial cups. During this interval Io, made suspicious by the absence of Sugiura, asked where he was. She was informed that immediately after greeting the bride he had borrowed Sadakata's horse and ridden off somewhere.

'After a while Sugiura returned and sat down in front of Io and Sadakata. Mopping his sweat-covered brow he said: "I can't apologize enough for my terrible mistake. As you know, I did exactly as you instructed me. I sent them word that I wished to call on them, and they replied that they would of course be pleased to receive me, and so I went. The beautiful woman I described to you was the one who came into the drawing room with the tea, sat down in front of me and formally welcomed me. True, I did see the one that arrived today, too, but she just stepped into the room carrying a bowl of sweets or something and instantly withdrew. I had no idea that that was Miss Teru. I was so taken aback when I saw her today that I borrowed your horse and rushed over to the Ōsu house to ask what had happened. Their explanation was that the woman who welcomed me was Ōsu's daughter-in-law who was there to introduce Miss Teru to me. I've been an utter fool." Sugiura then mopped his brow again.

'Io's face was flushed with anger as Sugiura Kizaemon finished telling his story. She turned to Sadakata and said, "What will you do?"

'Sugiura, with tears in his eyes, said: "I see no choice, sir, but for you to cancel the engagement. All I needed to do when I was there was simply to ask that other woman if she was Miss Teru. What a fool I was."

'Sadakata unfolded his arms and said: "Elder sister, there's no need for you to be upset. And you, Sugiwara, stop blaming yourself. I'm going through with the marriage. I'm not afraid of Ōsu, but I'm not anxious to start a quarrel with him either. Besides, it would be unseemly at my age to be too concerned about a woman's looks."

'And so Sadakata and Teru were married. Teru was born in 1835, and was thirty-one at the time of her marriage. Presumably she had not married earlier because she was ugly. After their marriage Sadakata did not associate much with members of her family outside of formal occasions, except that he soon came to love her younger brother Gentaku. This Gentaku was a good student, but neither his father nor his elder brother showed any inclination to encourage him in his studies; and it was Sadakata who would buy books for him, among which were some big ones like the 130-volume Yao printing of Ssu-ma Ch'ien's *Shih Chi* (Historical Records).'[6]

What Ōgai does not tell us is that according to Tamotsu, while Sadakata accepted his predicament as an expression of "Heaven's will," Io was adamant that he should cancel the engagement.[7] I suppose Ōgai wanted to retain for Io a modicum of ladylike passivity.

The impression one has is that Io had as much to say about Sadakata's affairs as he had about hers; and that generally, whatever disadvantages she might have suffered as a widow, she was not as isolated socially or housebound as one might have imagined. She gave parties, she was invited to those that others gave, and remarkably enough, we see her even going to a restaurant with another woman, accompanied by her young son Tamotsu.

Ōgai thinks that the incident about to be described probably took place in 1862, when Io was forty-six and Tamotsu five. But it is pretty certain that the time was the spring of 1865, when both were three years older.[8] "Otatsu" mentioned here was a former courtesan turned mistress and accomplice of a notorious robber of the time named Aoki Yatarō.

'One day Tamotsu went with his mother to Kakuonji Temple in Asakusa Nagasumi-chō. This was the family temple of the Yamanouchi. Afterward, as they were returning home along Kuramae-dōri, they chanced to meet in front of the Momotarō Cake Shop a woman whom Io knew. This woman had served in the upper Tōdō mansion when Io was also there, and like Io had been an attendant of the middle rank. Anxious to talk to this woman whom she had not seen for some time, Io took her to a famous restaurant nearby called Tagasode. Tamotsu accompanied them. . . .

'The room adjoining the one they were shown to seemed occupied by a large company of people. Yet there were no sounds of loud talking, let alone of singing and samisen playing. After a while, however, there was sudden activity in the room. Voices were raised in seeming agitation, then there was the sound of footsteps of numerous people scurrying out of the room. After that there was complete silence.

'When the serving woman came into their room Io asked what the excitement had been all about. "Those gentlemen were all rice brokers," the woman said, "and they were gambling when Otatsu burst into the room. The gentlemen ran away, leaving their money scattered all over the floor. Otatsu picked it up and left."

'Just as the woman had finished telling the story the door opened and an outlandish-looking man wearing two swords walked in. "I bet you were gambling with those fellows," he said menacingly, drawing his long sword. "If you have any money, get it out and put it down on the floor."

'"You damned fraud!" Io shouted, and drawing her dagger stood up. Losing all his initial bluster the man turned tail and ran out.'[9]

For whatever reason, Ōgai neglects to include the last part of Tamotsu's account of this incident. Perhaps he thought it was redundant. According to Tamotsu, he later asked his mother why she had done such a dangerous thing. He was of course very frightened. Her reply was that the fellow was just trying to scare them, thinking that three women and a child were easy prey. The best thing to do with fellows like that, she said, was to scare them out of their wits by doing something they never imagined you would do; if you sat around quivering and let them think you were helpless, they really might try to hurt you.[10]

8 *The Recall to Hirosaki*

In 1867 the Tsugaru authorities announced their decision to recall the domainal retainers and their families residing in Edo to Hirosaki. To gather all available manpower in Hirosaki, to unburden the domain of the prohibitive cost of maintaining a large contingent in Edo, to free themselves of ties with the Shogunate when its future was becoming increasingly uncertain, and from a safe distance watch the way the wind blew—these were some of the reasons for their decision. It had taken them ten years to reach it since Chūsai's advocacy of such a move.

For many people like Io the recall meant leaving their native city, where they had lived all their lives, for a remote provincial castle town they had never seen and thought they never would see. Even Chūsai in all his years of service had gone there only twice—the first time from 1833 to 1834, and the second time from 1837 to 1839—and it was probably more than the cold there that caused him to start drinking. And we remember what the late Lord Tsugaru Nobuyuki (he died in 1862) thought of the "mountain apes" of his domainal seat. In his abhorrence of Hirosaki, he was only being a typical native of Edo, for whom the mere thought of living anywhere else was barbarous. With what pain Io faced the prospect of leaving Edo and possibly never coming back to it, we can imagine. She and the children had to go, of course: had they stayed behind in Edo, they would no longer have

Io's journey from Edo to Hirosaki

belonged to the Tsugaru domain, and Tamotsu, who as head of the Shibue house was already a Tsugaru retainer, would have been without status.

Io had to wait until the following year, 1868, to leave Edo. And by the time she began to prepare for her departure, the Shogunal forces had been beaten badly at Toba and Fushimi—this was in January of that year—and Edo was soon to fall to the Imperial forces. In the northeast, between Edo and Hirosaki, pro-Shogunate lords and their men were rallying for the final stand against them. The Tsugaru domain had not yet declared for the Emperor, but it would do so in August of that year. In the passage quoted below, Ōgai mistakenly states that by the first of June, when Io left Edo, it had already done so. It was nevertheless not the best of times for a Tsugaru woman and her children to be traveling north from Edo.[1]

'The Shibue family sold their house and grounds, covering an area of 3,000 *tsubo* [about two and a half acres], for forty-five ryō. . . . In the garden still stood the tamarisk loved by Chūsai and his father. In the fire in Kanda Otamagaike the trunk had split in two. But though one of the split sides of the trunk was dead, the tree had survived the move from Kanda to Daidokoro-chō, and from Daidokoro-chō to Kamezawa-chō. There was also the stone lantern that Io's father had bequeathed to her. The thought of having to part with them was hard to bear. But to have a large tree and stone lantern transported for 182 *ri* [nearly 450 miles] would have been a major undertaking even for a prince. Besides, theirs was to be a journey in a time of turbulence, when one's own safety was by no means assured. They had no choice but to leave them where they stood.

'The "guests" in the house left, seeking relations in Edo or its environs who might give them shelter. The servants, except the two menservants who were to accompany the family to Hirosaki, were all let go. At such times the most pitiable are old people who are left homeless. Maki, who had come to them from the

Yamanouchi house, had died two years before; but the lay nun Myōryō-ni was still with them.

'Myōryō-ni had many relations in Edo, but none of them expressed willingness to accept her as their ward. For a time, then, Io was in a quandary as to what was to be done with her. . . . The woman had been born in 1781, and was now eighty-seven years old. She had once served in one of the Tsugaru mansions, but in all her life had never set foot outside of Edo. She was, in other words, much too old and feeble to undertake a long journey to a strange place where she knew no one. For both Io's and her own sake, she had to be left behind. . . .

'Myōryō-ni's closest relation was her younger brother who was a mortar dealer in Honjo Aioi-chō. This man refused to accept responsibility for her when the Shibue were about to leave Edo. So did her other shopkeeper relations in Edo, such as the family that sold candy in Imagawabashi, another that sold nails in Ishihara, another that sold cloth in Hakozaki, and another that sold socks in Toshima-chō.

'There was, however, a niece of hers who was married to one Tomita Jūbei, a caretaker at a temple in Nirayama in Izu Province; and when this woman talked to her husband about her aunt, he agreed without hesitation to have her come and live with them.

'On the twenty-second of May [in 1868] the Shibue left their house in Kamezawa-chō and moved into the lower Tsugaru mansion in Honjo Yokogawa. They left Edo on the first of June. This was the day when the Imperial forces occupied Edo Castle.

'The Shibue party, eight in number, consisted of Tamotsu, head of the family, aged eleven; his mother Io, aged fifty-two; her daughter Kuga, aged twenty-one; her daughter Miki, aged fifteen; her son Osamu, aged fourteen; Yajima Yutaka, aged thirty-three; and two menservants, one a man from Hirosaki, by name Iwasaki Komagorō, and the other a man from Tsuchiura in Hitachi Province, by name Chūjō Katsujirō.

'Traveling with them were Yakawa Bun'ichirō [a Tsugaru bushi] and the Asagoe family. Seven years previously, at the age of twenty, Bun'ichirō had married a woman named Ryū, daughter of a hardware dealer in Honjo Futatsume, and they had a son. When the Tsugaru bushi were ordered to return to Hirosaki, Ryū, loath to leave Edo, went back to her family with their son. . . . [This Bun'ichirō had been kind to Tamotsu when Tamotsu was first appointed page to Lord Nobuyuki in 1860. He was later to marry Kuga.]

'The Asagoe family consisted of man and wife and their daughter. They were accompanied by one manservant. The man Asagoe went by the personal professional name of Genryū, and was a physician of the outer chambers carrying a stipend of 180 koku.

'He was a profligate when a youth and was disowned by his father Eiju. Upon Eiju's death, however, he was reinstated as a "posthumous" adopted son and succeeded to the headship of the family. He then became a pupil of Shibue Chūsai, and through Chūsai's introduction was admitted to Kaiho Gyoson's academy. . . . He had since become close to the Shibue family. Born in 1838, he was thirty at the time of their departure from Edo. His wife Yoshi was twenty-three, and their daughter Fuku was not yet a year old.

'There was one man who was not permitted to leave Edo with the Shibue family despite his wish to do so. As I write about this I am made newly aware of how very different their society was from ours. That there were special ties between master and retainer, we know. What we perhaps do not know as well is that loyal and affectionate relationships were formed also between craftsmen or tradesmen and their patrons to whose houses they would regularly bring their specialties. Of the craftsmen who frequently came to the Shibue house, there was a maker of personal ornaments by the name of Chōhachi; and of the tradesmen, there was a sushi man by the name of Kyūjirō. Chōhachi had long been dead when the Shibue left Edo, but Kyūjirō was still alive at the age of sixty-five.

'The relationship of Chōhachi the ornament-maker to the Shibue was not simply that of visiting craftsman. It was in 1839, just after Chūsai had returned from Hirosaki, that Chōhachi, who was ill at the time, came to him for treatment. On learning that because of his illness Chōhachi was not able to practice his craft and he and his family were destitute, Chūsai put them up in the servants' quarters and gave them food and clothing until Chōhachi was well enough to start working again. Chōhachi never forgot Chūsai's kindness. He was present at Chūsai's funeral to assist the family with the arrangements. When he returned home that evening he had his customary cup of sake, then said to his wife: "Now that master Chūsai has died, I think it's perhaps time for me to go too." He later went upstairs to go to bed. The next morning he did not come down. When his wife went up to see what was the matter, she found him dead.

'Kyūjirō the sushi man had originally been a street fish vendor, and it was Io's elder brother Eijirō who, taking a liking to him, gave him the necessary capital to set up a restaurant. He was deft with the fish slicer, and soon his sushi became rather well thought of. He married a woman about ten years his junior, and in 1835 had a son who was named Toyokichi. Kyūjirō, born in 1803, was at the time thirty-two. When Io married Chūsai nine years later he began to deliver sushi to the Shibue house and in time became close to the family.

'When the Shibue began preparing for their departure from Edo, Kyūjirō earnestly pleaded with them to let him accompany them. He would come by himself, he said; his wife would be well looked-after by their son Toyokichi, now thirty-three. It would seem that part of his reason for wanting to go was entrepreneurial, in that he apparently thought he would start a sushi shop in Hirosaki. But it was mostly through devotion to Io that this old man of sixty-five proposed to undertake a journey of almost two hundred ri. The Shibue felt they could not refuse him without good cause; so they took the matter up with the domainal authorities, who were reluctant to give their approval. Finally, on informal instruction from a senior official, Kōno Rokurō, Io told Kyūjirō that he could not accompany them. Kyūjirō was deeply disappointed. It so happened, however, that next year he fell ill and died.

ʿThe Shibue party and their companions boarded a flat-bottomed boat near Futatsume Bridge in Honjo, and by way of the rivers Tategawa, Nakagawa, and Tonegawa went to Shibamata, then to Nagareyama, and finally to Oyama. They had gone only twenty-one ri [about fifty miles], yet this lap of the journey took them five days.

ʿThe pro-Imperial party within the Tsugaru domain, led by Nishidate Kosei, had held sway; and the Tsugaru family, with their long-standing connections with the princely Kyoto family of Konoe, had declared for the Emperor. [As we have noted, this was not the case; but to the domains loyal to the Shogunate, Tsugaru was no doubt suspect.] For Io and the rest, this meant that their route through the northeast traversed enemy domains ["unfriendly domains" would be nearer the truth], the one exception being the Akita domain. Of the travelers, the least encumbered was Yakawa Bun'ichirō, who had no dependents with him; and Asagoe Genryū had with him only his wife and baby daughter, and a manservant. The Shibue party, on the other hand, was large, and included an elderly person and children. And so it was decided that the Shibue would travel at their own pace and the others precede them.

ʿThe Shibue women and children were put in five closed litters, and Yajima Yutaka and the two menservants led the party on foot. When they approached the post-station of Ishibashi they were met by sentries of the Sendai domain. Twenty gun-bearing soldiers from either side of the road surrounded the party, and opening the door of each litter examined the occupant closely. The women were allowed to proceed without much fuss, but Tamotsu was questioned thoroughly. That night at their lodging Io disguised him as a girl. [Tamotsu in particular presumably because as head of the house his survival was important; also, Osamu was probably too old to be disguised as a girl.]

ʿThe town of Yamagata in Dewa was ninety ri from Edo and

thus halfway to Hirosaki. It was the custom for travelers from Edo to Hirosaki to celebrate their arrival at this halfway point, but Io's party, not wanting to attract attention, avoided the inns and stayed quietly at an eel restaurant.

'The normal route from Yamagata to Hirosaki led over Kozaka Pass and through the castle town of Sendai. But Io's party decided to avoid Sendai, and instead go to Yonezawa by way of Itaya Pass. It turned out that this route was not safe either. When they reached Kaminoyama they learned that conditions ahead were not at all certain, and were forced to stay in the town for several days.[2]

'The money they had brought with them was now spent. Thinking it unwise to travel with too much money on them, they had put most of what they had in the bottom of some fifty chests that were to be shipped from Edo to Hirosaki. In Kaminoyama, then, they sold over half of the belongings that they had brought so far with such difficulty. They would have had to do so anyway, money or no money, for having chosen to avoid the main roads, they were constrained to travel as lightly as possible. Needless to say, the proceeds from the sale were insufficient to cover the cost of the rest of the journey. It was their good fortune that at this time they chanced to meet a man from the treasury of the Tsugaru domain, from whom Io was able to borrow a small sum.

'The road from Kaminoyama took them through sparsely populated and mountainous country. There were times when they had to descend and ascend precipices by rope ladders; and often they spent the night at small resting places along the road that provided merely rice-cake and tea. On several nights they were robbed.

'As they went over Innai Pass and entered the Akita domain they felt some relief, for the lord of the domain, Satake Yoshitaka, like their own lord Tsugaru Tsuguakira, had joined the Imperial cause. They passed through the domain safely.

'Next they had to go over Yatake Pass and cross the so-called Forty-Eight Rivers to reach Hirosaki. The watershed on Yatake Pass was the border between Lord Satake's domain and Lord

Tsugaru's. A little way down from here was a barrier station with guards. It was only after these guards had examined the Shibue party's travel permits that they at last became civil. And when one of them pointed at the peak of Mount Iwaki towering above the clouds and said that that was the Tsugaru Fuji and that at its foot lay the castle town of Hirosaki, Io and the others were so thankful they could not hold back their tears.'³

We learn from Tamotsu's memoirs, not from Ōgai's text, that their journey of 450 miles ended thirty-two days after they left Edo.⁴ One is surprised that it did not take longer, considering that they did not use the main highway always or ride in horse-drawn carriages. And even if most of the traveling was done in litters (borne on the shoulders of two men going at a trot), it must have been utterly exhausting. No wonder they were so glad to see Mount Iwaki.

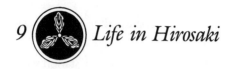 *Life in Hirosaki*

Hirosaki could hardly have been a welcome change from Edo. Io and her family had been transplanted from a city of over one million people, no doubt one of the most sophisticated in the world then, to a provincial town of some thirty-five thousand situated in the northernmost part of the main island. Only exile to Hokkaido would have seemed worse.

To the townspeople of Hirosaki, Io and her children, with their elegant big-city clothes, their refined speech and manners, were objects of unabashed curiosity. "Hey, you Edo folk!" they would call to the exiles whenever they ventured out. Tamotsu possessed a Western-style, black cloth umbrella. If he happened to go out with it, a rare commodity even in Edo at the time, he would soon be surrounded by a gaping crowd. His pocket watch was broken in a matter of days through handling by strangers who, having heard about it, came to his lodgings to inspect it.

To the exiles from the big city, the local people must have seemed equally foreign. With his penchant for understatement and oblique reference, Ōgai tells us that these people gathered up their hair with hemp yarn and wore clothes made of locally woven coarse cotton. He might have mentioned also that they spoke in a dialect which to Io would often not have sounded like Japanese at all; or that their food and eating habits would have been very different from what she had been accustomed to; or that what they regarded as good theater would have seemed to Io quite barbaric. The list could go on.

It is always tempting to caricature provincials when describing them from the point of view of those from the city; and it is to Ōgai's credit that he avoids the temptation. Yet in refusing to be more informative about what it must have been like for Io to begin a new life at her age among people so different from herself, Ōgai, I think, is being too reticent.

Lack of sophistication aside, Ōgai leaves no doubt in our minds as to the kind of mean, superstitious parochialism that existed in Hirosaki.

'A most unexpected thing happened to Chūjō Katsujirō, one of the two Shibue menservants.

'Two or three months after the Shibue arrived in Hirosaki there was a rainstorm. It was the belief of the people of the Tsugaru domain that when outsiders came and settled amongst them the deity of Mount Iwaki in retribution would cause a rainstorm. For this reason, apparently, the local people regarded outsiders who came to live in the domain as a curse. Of the outsiders, the ones that angered the deity most were those from Tango [an area to the north of Kyoto] and those from Nanbu [an area to the southeast of Hirosaki]. The reason why the Tango people were marked for such special attention was this: the deity was in fact Hirosaki's own Lady Anju of the old local legend, who had been so ill-used by Sanshō Dayū, a magnate of Tango. As for Lady Anju's dislike of the Nanbu people, the reason is obscure. Perhaps her selectivity in this particular instance was influenced by the wishes of her followers.

'Some days after the rainstorm those families who had recently arrived from Edo were instructed to determine upon thorough examination the places of origin of all 'outsiders' in their households. If they were from Nanbu or Tango or were of uncertain origin, they were to be expelled from the domain. The man in the Shibue household marked for suspicion by the authorities was Chūjō. And when his statement that he had been born in Hitachi was submitted to them, they refused to believe it and declared that his birthplace was undetermined. Io had no choice but to give him travel money and send him back to Tokyo.[1]

Such arbitrariness on the part of the domainal authorities may be understood as an expression of natural suspiciousness in a time of uncertainty. The Tsugaru domain was now at war with pro-Shogunate forces to the north (in Hokkaido) and south of them; and although there was little doubt they had chosen the right side—just in the nick of time, for the fighting in northern Japan ended only three months after they unequivocally joined the Imperial side—they were not at all certain what the future of the domain would be under the new regime. To be as well prepared as possible for any contingency after the cessation of war—economically, politically, and militarily—was of course their overriding concern. They would soon decrease drastically the hereditary stipends of all the retainers, so that the domainal treasury would have a greater reserve. And until the abolition in 1871 of the domainal system throughout Japan, they made it very difficult for retainers to leave Tsugaru, lest domainal manpower be seriously reduced. They were in a highly nervous, protective frame of mind, watchful of all potential threats to domainal unity and security. That the traditional parochialism of Tsugaru, the suspicion of all outsiders, should have become exacerbated at this time is not surprising.

Whether the expulsion of Chūjō Katsujirō from the domain can be seen as an indignity to Io, as a sign of her helplessness in Hirosaki, we are not sure. But she was a widow, of a family whose head, Tamotsu, was still only eleven years old and serving as a page at the castle. On an allowance that covered only the cost of food and lodging, she and her family lived in rooms in a house belonging to a second-hand clothes dealer. She was perhaps not destitute, but one would surmise that she was hardly a person of consequence in Hirosaki. Unluckily, for well over a year after her arrival in Hirosaki, she had to manage without the protection and support of Hirano Sadakata, the only male relation of substance she had.

Sadakata and his family were of the last group of Tsugaru families to leave Edo. His party, comprising about thirty families, had set sail from Edo on a newly built domainal ship, the *Ansai-maru,* a month or so after Io's departure. They had not made much headway when the ship's steering gear failed. They had had to return to Edo by land, and wait for another ship to take them to their domain. By the time Sadakata arrived in Aomori, then a small harbor town in Tsugaru, it was January of 1870, a year and a half after he had originally left Edo.

The note Io received from Sadakata in Aomori saying that he was stranded there without funds was the first piece of communication she had had from him in all these months. It is scarcely believable that the domainal authorities could not have advanced him the money he needed to get him to Hirosaki from Aomori; but what we are told is that Io, having absolutely no money to spare, raised twenty-five ryō by pawning thirty-five of the swords she had had shipped in chests from Edo, and with this went to Aomori to fetch Sadakata. It is possible that Sadakata had recuperated in style in Aomori after his journey and got himself in debt. It is also possible that one reason why it took him so inordinately long to arrive in Tsugaru was that finding himself back in Edo after the failure of his first attempt to leave, he was in no hurry to make his second.

About a year before Sadakata's arrival—that is, in her first winter in Hirosaki—Io and her family were moved by the authorities to one of a row of attached houses recently put up in the outskirts of the town. Called *nagaya* in Japan, such houses were usually jerry-built, cramped, separated from one another by thin walls, and afforded little privacy. In the final version of his text Ōgai does not describe, or imagine for us, what it was like for Io to live in one of these. In an earlier version, however, he gives us a hint of the sadness of her new condition. He writes there that she and her family were constantly beset by trespassers consumed with curiosity. They would force their way through the fence, poke holes in the papered windows and peep. Others, even more shameless, would come right into the house to stare and ask questions. Some of them would come armed with flasks of sake, prepared for a long siege. These last were all native bushi, people with whom Io felt compelled to keep on good terms. "After such uninvited guests had departed," Ōgai writes, "she would pretend to be amused. But she could not hide her longing for her native city which by then had already been renamed Tokyo."[2]

Presumably these people would have been more circumspect had Io not been a widow. Ōgai makes a telling remark that the visitations would occur after Yajima Yutaka—still living with Io and now employed in a modest way as a doctor—had left for work.

To what extent her sense of helplessness in her new environment led her finally to consent to the marriage of Yakawa Bun'ichirō, the young bushi who had left Edo with them, to her daughter Kuga, we can only guess. But we do know that neither she nor Kuga was enthusiastic about the match, and that Io was afraid of the ill will their rejection of the proposal would cause.

Bun'ichirō was born in 1841 to a cadet branch of a family of hereditary master horsemen serving the Tsugaru lords.[3] When still a boy he lost his father; and then his mother remarried, leaving him in the care of priests at a temple with which the Tsugaru family had connections. Some years later, when he was about seventeen, he was taken into the main Yakawa house (not, we gather, as an adopted son). We are not told how he fared as a ward of the priests, or why the main family took so long to take him in. Nor do we know whether his childhood experiences had anything to do with his marked kindness toward the boy Tamotsu, who too was fatherless when he came to serve as a page under his supervision.

Unlike Hirano Sadakata, say, Bun'ichirō was not exactly an important bushi in his own right. But he was of a good soldierly lineage (he himself was now in the horse guards), and the main Yakawa family were of some consequence; so that Io, a widow, could not dismiss his suit, pressed with some persistence, too lightly. Besides, he was a friend of the family, known to them for years. (One of his aunts was married to Satake Eikai, the painter we remember for his ill-fated wooing of Io by the pond.)

Our impression of him is that while he was a friendly and pleasant enough person, he lacked distinction, and was somewhat erratic. We learn little about him from Ōgai, partly because, one suspects, he was rather ordinary, and partly because he was still alive when Ōgai was writing his book, and not everything known about him could be told without giving offense. Ōgai is not all reticence, however, when he tells this curious—and sad—story about an early love affair of his.

'Bun'ichirō was a fine figure of a man, and was rather aware of it. He became familiar with a prostitute in Yoshiwara and visited her frequently. In time he promised to marry her. One night on one of his visits he suddenly found himself awake, and when he turned to look at the woman lying next to him he saw that she was fast asleep with one eye wide open. Shocked by the terrible change in the face that he had always thought beautiful, and wondering whether he was not indeed seeing the face in a nightmare, he sat up. The woman now was awake too, and asked if anything was the matter. Before he was able to give a coherent reply she guessed what had happened. Her face contorted with shame, she · confessed that she had an artificial eye. In tears she begged him not to break his promise to marry her. Of course he wouldn't, he said, and went home. I am told that he did not go back to her again.'[4]

We remember that when Bun'ichirō left Edo with the Shibue, his wife chose to stay behind with their young son. What his wife had done, in effect, was to divorce him rather than accompany him to Hirosaki. Soon after arriving in Hirosaki Bun'ichirō married again, but this marriage quickly ended in divorce. Kuga, then, in marrying Bun'ichirō became his third wife. She, for her part, had received at least one proposal in Hirosaki, which was turned down, Ōgai informs us, mostly because of her own unwillingness. The truth of the matter seems to be that she really did not want to get married. She was happy enough to live at home with her mother, her sister, and her brothers, and is quoted—though not by Ōgai—as saying, "I'm not ready to be ordered about by a husband."[5]

Whatever Kuga's memories of Io's treatment of her as a child might have been, she clearly preferred being with her mother to being a wife; and there is little doubt that had Io not felt so pressured by certain social obligations, she would have supported her daughter in her unwillingness to marry, though presumably not forever.

Io did not love Kuga as she had loved Tō, the girl who died of smallpox, or as she loved Tamotsu, her youngest son. But there was the bond between them of two women who had much in common—pride, intelligence, resourcefulness, and their refusal to play the docile woman. Later, when Io, her two daughters, and Bun'ichirō had returned to Tokyo—and here I am anticipating—Kuga opened a sweet shop to support herself and her husband, who was unsuccessful in his incongruous attempt at being a pawnbroker. (By then the bushi had lost their hereditary privileges, and like so many of his kind, Bun'ichirō simply was not cut out to be an entrepreneur, on any scale.) One day, at a storytellers' hall, Io and Tamotsu heard one of the storytellers in his prefatory remarks express admiration for a certain lady, the daughter of a once prominent family, making a living as the mistress of a sweet shop. He was of course talking about Kuga. We are told that on hearing this mention of her daughter Io was hardly able to contain her emotion.

The marriage took place on the nineteenth of October, 1869. Kuga was at the time twenty-two, and Bun'ichirō, twenty-eight. Ōgai writes:

'It was probably after his return from Hakodate [in Hokkaido, where he had been in the fighting] that Bun'ichirō, deciding that he wanted to marry Kuga, made known his wish to the Shibue several times through intermediaries. But the Shibue were not quick to respond. Kuga was as ever reluctant to get married; and Io, though long aware that Bun'ichirō was a well-intentioned man, had no desire to have him as a son-in-law. And so for some time the relationship between the two families was strained.

'Bun'ichirō in his prime was a passionate man; and he was so ardent in his suit that the Shibue became deeply concerned about their future relationship with him were they to continue to demur. One might say, then, that in finally marrying him Kuga was the victim of this concern.

'Nominally Kuga married into the Yakawa family; but in practice it was as if Bun'ichirō had married into hers, for from the day of the wedding, the couple spent entire days in the Shibue house and went back to their own house only to sleep.'[6]

Kuga gave birth to a son the next year, but this child soon died. The marriage itself lasted less than four years. They were divorced in 1873, at about the same time that Kuga closed down her sweet shop, which apparently had failed to provide sufficient income for the two of them. It was after this that she resolved to support herself as a nagauta singer and teacher. She did not marry again.

Kuga's younger sister Miki, too, was married while the Shibue were in Hirosaki. This was in 1870, when Miki was seventeen. Her marriage, alas, was something of a farce. Soon after the wedding Yajima Shūtei, the doctor who had replaced Yutaka as the head of the Yajima house, informed Io that the marriage could not possibly be consummated, due to the bridegroom's "physical incapacity." "Io had no choice," Ōgai tells us, "but to recall Miki."[7] The reader may wonder how Shūtei came to have such information. The answer is simple: he was the bridegroom's family doctor.[8]

Shūtei, as a Tsugaru retainer, had come to Hirosaki in 1868. Tetsu, whom Shūtei had reluctantly agreed to have in his house in Edo, must have come with him; for she was living with him in Hirosaki in November of 1869 when Yutaka, still living with Io, was at last persuaded to reunite with his wife.

Whatever our opinion of Yutaka may be, there is no denying that Tetsu had every reason to be bitter about her life. She had been made ugly by smallpox and left an orphan as a child; she had then been married to a hopelessly errant man who not only deserted her but lost for her her birthright as a Yajima to a stranger, on whose grudging charity she was now completely dependent. It was Shūtei who now had her father's rank as physician of the outer chambers. Her own husband Yutaka, having been forced to retire prematurely and in disgrace as head of the house, was virtually statusless, which meant that she was too. If she turned out to be an unpleasant woman—and according to Ōgai, she did indeed—we can hardly blame her.

'In the month that followed Kuga's marriage to Bun'ichirō, Yajima Yutaka acquired a house in Dote-machi [a neighborhood in Hirosaki] and recalled his wife Tetsu, who had been living under Shūtei's care. This was under the circumstances the proper thing for Yutaka to do, and their reunion was in no small measure due to Io's efforts. But Tetsu, now twenty-three, was not the easily coaxable child she had been earlier in their marriage; and the house in Dote-machi became the scene of much turmoil which finally led to a crisis in Yutaka's life.

'That between the two no conjugal love would come to exist was to be expected. The problem, then, was not that there was no love between them, but that they soon became sworn enemies. And in their quarrels, it was always Tetsu who took the offensive. The accusation she tirelessly hurled at him was that he had led them to their present state of penury. "If you hadn't been so feeble," she would say, "we wouldn't have lost everything to that Shūtei fellow!" When Yutaka then would try to remonstrate, she would sneer and click her tongue in derision.

'Day after day, week after week, the quarreling went on. Io and others tried in every way they could to bring about peace between the two, but without success.

'In desperation Io finally appealed to Shūtei to take Tetsu back into his house, but he would not hear of it. Time and time again she repeated her appeal, only to be rebuffed by Shūtei, until the exchange of appeal and rebuff began to take on the character of an endless ritual.

'And then on the twenty-ninth of January of the following year Yutaka suddenly disappeared. Thinking that he had gone out to seek relief from his misery in some house of pleasure, the Shibue had men go out to look for him in the most likely establishments, but he was nowhere to be found. . . .

'He was not heard from until the afternoon of the second of February, when a man from Ishikawa, a post-station on the highway, came to deliver two letters from him, one addressed to Io and the other to Tamotsu. They had been written on the day he left his house. Both were letters of farewell, stained here and there with tears. Ishikawa was no further than three and a half miles from Hirosaki, but that was little consolation, for Yutaka had seen to it that the letters were delivered after he had left Ishikawa.

'Io and Tamotsu were filled with concern for Yutaka's safety. How could he cope with the snow-covered roads? What if he were to fall ill during his journey? And so again they hired men to search for him. Tamotsu himself braved the snow and went to various towns outside of Hirosaki such as Ishikawa, Ōwani, Kuradate, and Ikarigaseki to make inquiries, but he learned nothing. Yutaka had disappeared without a trace.

'Later it transpired that Yutaka had headed for Tokyo, where he arrived on the twenty-first of February. He sought and found refuge in a restaurant in Yoshiwara called Minato-ya, the madame of which establishment he knew well. She was a woman of considerable maturity who always addressed Yutaka affectionately as "Chō-san" [or Mr. Butterfly, *chō* being one of the characters he had used in his professional name during his stint in the music hall].

'In Minato-ya previously there had been a serving girl named Mina, who because of her beauty was the chief attraction of the establishment. She took as her patron a certain man named Kōno . . . who eventually married her. When Yutaka arrived in Tokyo she had opened a geisha house by the river at Imado-bashi. This, too, was named Minato-ya.

'With the sponsorship of Minato-ya in Yoshiwara, then, Yutaka set himself up in Sanyabori as a geisha escort, getting most of his business from the geishas of Minato-ya in Imado-bashi. [The Japanese word for Yutaka's new occupation was *hakoya,* or "box man," for the reason that when a geisha was called to a restaurant from her geisha house to entertain customers, the hakoya would accompany her, carrying her samisen and whatever else she would need in a box.]

'After being in the business for about four and a half months he married the widow of an antique dealer, thanks to the good offices of a certain man he knew. The widow's name was Masa, and her late husband's name was Reisuke. The shop was called Yasuda. Yutaka's career as an antique dealer, however, was even more short-lived than that as a box man, for not long after marrying him Masa died.

'In the meantime Shioda Ryōsan [his old boon companion], for some time a bureaucrat in Urawa Prefecture, had risen in the bureaucracy and was at this time a civil magistrate. Ryōsan now recommended Yutaka to the prefectural governor, who on the thirteenth of September appointed him a clerk in the office of prison administration. Yutaka was at the time thirty-five.'⁹

The end of this chapter of Yutaka's life, then, is near-comedy. Ōgai of course does not belabor the incongruousness of Ryōsan's being a civil magistrate, or of Yutaka's being appointed to the office of prison administration on Ryōsan's recommendation, after having recently been a box man, and then a widow's kept man (which in fact he was, despite Ōgai's polite use of the word *marry*). But there is no questioning Ōgai's appreciation of Yutaka's ability to rise above pathos, to retain that dignity peculiar to comic heroes.

In defense of the prefectural governor's seemingly eccentric choice of personnel, one should say that the prefecture as a regional administrative unit was just being introduced, and its appointment procedures, especially at the lower levels, were still pretty haphazard.[10] Besides, both Ryōsan and Yutaka were well-educated men, and no doubt worldly enough to perform their respective duties with some semblance of assurance. One might add too that the position Yutaka was appointed to ranked very low in the bureaucratic hierarchy, and he was not to rise much higher.

From his solicitousness toward Io later, when she returned to Tokyo, one would surmise that in Hirosaki he was no less a friend to her; and surely it must have been a comfort to her that when Yutaka disappeared, Sadakata had just arrived. Without either, she would have been without the companionship of an adult male relation who was close to her. There was Yakawa Bun'ichirō, her son-in-law; but we have no indication that she felt more than a casual fondness for him, or that he felt any differently toward her.

Of her two young sons, Tamotsu, the younger but the heir, was clearly her favorite: he was by now the more serious, the more intellectually inclined, the one that Io depended on to maintain the distinction of the Shibue house. But Osamu certainly was not dim-witted, and it is possible that had he been given more encouragement as a child, had he been made the heir on the strength of his seniority, he might indeed have turned out to be a more studious youth. At any rate, when Io and her family arrived in Hirosaki, she had been sure for some time of her elder son's disinclination to become a scholar.

'Of concern to Io at this time was the education of Osamu. He was not like Tamotsu, who needed no prompting from others to read, and who moreover could be trusted to pick the right books. Thus when Tamotsu started studying the Chinese classics under the tutelage of Kanematsu Sekkyo [1810–77; one of the most prominent Confucian scholars in Hirosaki],[11] Io was content to leave him absolutely alone. Whether he chose to become a Confucian scholar, or whether he chose to become a doctor, in either case he could pass muster. Osamu, on the other hand, disliked books. When confronted with them he would immediately question their practicality. Forced to conclude therefore that he lacked the makings of a scholar, Io decided to have him begin in earnest the study of medicine.

'When she was settled in Hirosaki she embarked on a search for the right doctor to teach Osamu, and was fortunate to have her son accepted as a pupil by Ono Genshū, personal physician to Lord Tsugaru Tsuguakira.

'Ono Genshū was the second son of Tsushima Ikujirō, a bushi of the Hirosaki domain. His boyhood name was Tsunekichi. One night when he was about fifteen, his father Ikujirō suddenly became ill. Tsunekichi ran through the dark streets to a certain doctor's house. But although the doctor was in, he refused to come with Tsunekichi to look at his father. The distress he felt then, the bitterness of that experience, remained with Tsunekichi all his life. And it was for this reason, apparently, that when he later became a doctor, he would willingly go to the house of any sick person, no matter how poor that person might be, or how far the house, or how inconvenient the time. At the age of twenty-five he became the adopted son of one Ono Shūtoku of the same domain, and married Ono's eldest daughter Sono.

'Genshū, then, was a selfless and upright man. When he became physician to Lord Tsugaru, he would arrive at his place of duty in the morning before the others and be the last to leave in the evening. During his off-duty hours he would care for the sick, whether bushi or commoner, ungrudgingly and tirelessly.

'Kudō Tazan, professor at Keikoku-kan [the domainal school for Confucian studies] and founder of a private academy in Go-jūkoku-chō, was a friend of Genshū's. Their friendship had begun when Tazan, yet without a domainal appointment [and therefore without a steady income] was Genshū's patient. Aware of Tazan's poverty, Genshū had treated him with care, expecting and receiving no fees. Mr. Tonosaki, a son of Tazan's [now living in Hirosaki], knew Genshū, and reports that he was a man of warmth and quiet charm, with not a touch of meanness in him. He was indeed a "prize catch" for Io. . . .

'And so it was a fine teacher that Osamu was provided with; yet the sad fact is that Osamu himself had no desire to become a doctor. And the people of Hirosaki began to see him running about the fields, his head shaved as befitted a prospective doctor, dressed in a Western-style shirt and short Japanese trousers, a red blanket draped around his shoulders, and carrying a gun—in other words, imitating a domainal foot soldier of the time.'[12]

With what dismay Io watched her son rushing out of the house in his strange costume, we can well imagine. But if there were altercations between the two, we are not told of them. Perhaps by then Io was quite resigned to Osamu's obstinate preference for the ordinary.

Osamu soon gave up his medical studies altogether, and enrolled in a class that taught "foreign arithmetic and bookkeeping." Meanwhile the foot soldiers whose company he tirelessly sought came to rather like him, and adopted him as a kind of mascot, nicknaming him "the fighting doctor." Their goodwill was not without practical result, it would seem, for in June of 1870 Osamu was appointed a trainee for the newly constituted military band.

Osamu was not to remain a prospective military bandsman for long, however. Later that year, he became the adopted son of one Yamada Gengo, a guard at the Tsugaru mansion in Honjo Yokogawa in Tokyo, and left for that city. That under normal circumstances Io would not have agreed to such an alliance, there is no question. Gengo was hardly more than a watchman, and was near the bottom of the hierarchy of Tsugaru retainers. But circumstances had indeed changed drastically for the Shibue that year, as we shall soon see. Besides, Osamu himself seemed bent on an undistinguished career, and being Gengo's adopted son would at least assure him of a hereditary position within the hierarchy. And perhaps a more important consideration was that through Osamu the Shibue would establish a foothold in Tokyo.

On July 16, 1870, the domainal authorities announced their decision to reduce substantially the stipends of the Tsugaru retainers, expressed still in rice amounts, but as *hyō*, or sacks of rice, hyō being roughly equivalent to the net value of koku. At the same time that they announced these reductions, which were calculated more or less equitably according to the original stipends, the authorities introduced a new system of classification of the *shi*, or the gentry, into three main classes according to their new hyō stipends—the upper, the middle, and the lower; and these main classes were then subdivided into two, the upper and the lower. If one's new stipend were 20 hyō, for example, one would be a lower lower shi; if 40 hyō, a lower middle shi; if 80 hyō, an upper middle shi; if 150 hyō, a lower upper shi. Now, the Shibue, on the basis of their former stipend, should have been placed in the 80 hyō bracket under the new dispensation and classified as upper middle shi, which was more or less where they had belonged in the old hierarchy. But they were not.[13]

What happened was that doctors of the domain were treated differently from the others, and made subject to a discriminatory clause that in effect downgraded them as a class; so that the Shibue, instead of being granted 80 hyō, were granted 30 hyō, and thus placed in the upper lower class in the hierarchy. And when they expressed their dissatisfaction to the authorities, not only were they unheeded but were reminded that as doctors, even their claim to being gentry at all was questionable.

The interesting thing is that the basis of Tamotsu's—and no doubt Io's—complaint was not so much that the demotion of doctors of the domain was unjust, as that the Shibue were *scholar*-doctors, and as scholars they were not subject to the discriminatory clause. (We remember that in choosing medicine as a career for her son Osamu, Io herself was acknowledging the inferior status of doctoring per se. The ordinary practice of medicine verged on being a trade; while the pursuit of classical learning, which her other son Tamotsu was engaged in, whether he was to become a doctor or not, was a more dignified and gentlemanly occupation, worthy of her late husband's heir.)

The authorities clearly were not wrong in classifying the Shibue as doctors; nor, however, were the Shibue wrong in emphasizing their identity as a scholarly family. The most we can say about the matter is that perhaps the Shibue were being less whimsical than their superiors, especially in view of the fact that at just about this time, Tamotsu was appointed assistant instructor in classics at the domainal academy; and that had they not been an Edo family recently come to Hirosaki, they might have been treated more generously.

It was after the reduction in their stipend and their demotion that Tamotsu, seeing that the future held little for him in Hirosaki, resolved to return to Tokyo and try to prepare himself for a new career there. Io's agreement to have Osamu adopted by so humbly placed a man as Yamada Gengo, then, may be seen not only as an acknowledgment on her part of her own family's decline, but as a move in anticipation of the eventual departure for Tokyo of Tamotsu and of the rest of the family. That Yamada Gengo had once been a Tsugaru bushi of substance must have consoled Io a little, though it cannot have weighed too heavily in her decision to permit the adoption. Ōgai writes:

'Sometime in the Tenpō Era [1830–43] when Tsugaru Nobuyuki was still lord of the domain, Gengo, then serving as a secretary of the inner chambers, incurred Lord Nobuyuki's displeasure by an act of disobedience and was dismissed from office. Desiring neither to serve another lord nor to enter trade, he rented a room in Fugenji, his family temple, in Honjo Nakanogō, and going out into the streets every day earned what money he could as a mendicant singer.

'This life of sheer destitution lasted about thirty years; yet throughout this period he kept his swords and his crested, formal bushi's clothes in a wicker chest.

'Then in 1870, Lord Tsugaru Tsuguakira recalled him and appointed him a retainer of low rank [*memie-ika,* that is, not entitled to an audience with his lord] with a stipend of twenty hyō, his duty being guard at the Tsugaru mansion in Honjo Yokogawa. But now old and in ill health, Gengo knew that he would not be able for long to remain in active service; and so he sought to adopt a son to succeed him.

'Gengo had a relation in Hirosaki by the name of Tozawa Isei who thought Osamu a good candidate for adoption. And in trying to persuade Io to agree to the arrangement this Tozawa pointed out that the Yamada family had not always been so lowly, that working in Tokyo would offer opportunities for advancement, and that Osamu's presence in Tokyo might prove convenient for Tamotsu when he decided to go there. Tozawa made this last point because he knew that Tamotsu, shamed by his demotion and the improportionate reduction in stipend, was at the time considering going to Tokyo to vindicate his honor.'[14]

Io liked and respected Tozawa, and Hirano Sadakata was in favor of the proposal; so the matter was settled. On the eighteenth of February, 1871 Osamu set sail from Aomori to join his new family in Tokyo; but he was never to meet the man whose son he had become, for Gengo died while Osamu was still at sea.

10   *Return to Tokyo*

Osamu left Hirosaki at a time when it was becoming increasingly difficult for Tsugaru retainers to do so. By 1871, the domainal authorities had become extremely nervous about the growing restlessness of the bushi who, like Tamotsu, were beginning to see little future for themselves in the small provincial castle town and to think of ways of escaping to Tokyo where, as Tozawa argued in the case of Osamu, opportunities for advancement were greater. The bushi as a class were an anachronism, as was the domainal system, and soon both would cease to exist. But in the meantime, the authorities were intent on preventing "desertion," as they called it, and were reluctant to permit anyone—at least anyone of real or potential consequence—to leave the domain. We remember that as early as 1868, an important Edo-based bushi of the domain, Hirakawa Hanji, had elected to remain in Edo at the time of the recall, surrendering his bushi status and becoming a rice merchant. However contemptible his action may have seemed to his fellow retainers, the fact is that his "desertion" showed some perspicacity on his part. A few years later, many would be wishing to follow his example. We are told that in 1871, bushi morality—meaning, among other things, aversion to money-making—had so declined that Io was approached several times by those of a mercenary bent who tried to coax her into investing in speculative business ventures. One proposition was that she buy the restaurant Nakamura-rō in Ryōgoku in Tokyo. An investment of one thousand ryō now, she was told, would be worth tens of thousands later. Another proposition was that she buy shares in a concern dealing in patent medicine; they could be bought cheap, and from the very day of her buying them she would start earning a monthly income of three to five hundred ryō. "Needless to say," Ōgai tells us, "Io refused to lend her ear to such suggestions."¹ (The sums mentioned here are very large, and one wonders whether Io indeed had access to such money. In view of the hardship experienced by Tamotsu in Tokyo later, one would say that she could not have. It is possible, of course, that she still had valuable personal possessions that could be sold for a lot of money in a time of emergency. But all indications are that from the time of her move to Hirosaki until her death in Tokyo, her condition was never much above that of genteel poverty.)

The domain had raised no objections to Osamu's leaving for Tokyo. His adoptive father was a Tokyo-based retainer, so there was no gainsaying the legitimacy of his reason for going there. And it would not be too unkind of us to think that he could hardly have been regarded as valuable human property of the domain. But Tamotsu was another matter. He was the head of the Shibue family, and not withstanding his recent demotion, he was recognized as a young man of talent, whose services would be of value to the domain. Moreover, his bitter resentment at his demotion was known to the authorities, so that his motives for leaving Hirosaki would be immediately suspect.

It was in early 1871 that Tamotsu began in earnest to prepare for his departure. His mentor Kanematsu Sekkyo, who was fond of him, had promised to try to obtain for him a domainal scholarship at some opportune time for study in Tokyo. But unwilling to wait indefinitely for such an eventuality, Tamotsu decided he would go at his own expense, and applied for permission to do so to Nishidate Kosei (1829–92), the senior administrator of the domain, who had sworn he would prevent the loss to the domain of "any man of parts."

That Tamotsu was willing to pay out of his own pocket for the cost of studying in Tokyo made him all the more suspect. For were he to go on a scholarship, he would be more easily under domainal control, and his good faith more assured. Nevertheless Nishidate was willing to give Tamotsu permission to go, *provided* that he went alone. His mother was to remain in Hirosaki; and should he in the midst of his studies express any desire to have his mother join him, it would be seen as a sign of bad faith, of disloyalty to the domain, and she would not be allowed to leave. In brief, Io was to remain in Hirosaki as a hostage.

The condition set by Nishidate could not have come as a surprise either to Tamotsu or Io. It is a measure of their courage and determination, in any case, that Tamotsu, hardly more than a boy then, should have resolved to go to the great city on his own to study, and that Io should have encouraged him to do so. It was not as though he was going away to boarding school, sure to come home for his holidays. Given the travel conditions of those days, the distance between Hirosaki and Tokyo was enormous. It was not certain if Tamotsu would ever return; nor was it any more certain that Io would ever be able to see Tokyo again. Yutaka had already gone, and so had Osamu; and now Tamotsu was to go. She must have felt terribly forlorn.

Tamotsu obtained permission to have a portion of the family stipend sent to him in Tokyo. For money he needed immediately, he sold about a third of his large collection of woodblock prints, including many by Utamaro and Hokusai. Of the proceeds, which came to approximately a hundred ryō, he kept half, and gave the other half to his mother.

'Of all the people he went to say goodbye to in Hirosaki, the two who were most saddened to see him go were Kanematsu Sekkyo and Hirai Tōdō [the expert calligrapher who had been Sadakata's colleague in the liaison office in Edo]. Tōdō had developed a lump under his left jaw, and had given himself the sobriquet "Ryū-ō" [meaning "old man with the lump"]. As he and Tamotsu parted he wept, saying that they would not meet again. In the following year, on the eighteenth of October, Tōdō died in his house in Shiowake-chō. He was fifty-eight. . . .

'Tamotsu formally resigned his position at the domainal academy; and on the tenth of May, 1871, he and his mother sat together and drank water out of a sake cup in farewell. They did so because they knew that under the circumstances, their parting might be permanent. Tamotsu was then fourteen and Io fifty-five. At the time of Chūsai's death Tamotsu had only been an infant. The true sorrow of parting of child and parent, he therefore now learned for the first time; and we are told that as the litter carried him away from the house, he was barely able to keep himself from sobbing.'[2]

Tamotsu arrived in Tokyo on the twenty-fifth of May, and was given quarters in the Tsugaru mansion in Honjo Futatsume. This was the domainal mansion as distinguished from Lord Tsugaru Tsuguakira's private mansion, also in Honjo, which was where Osamu, as successor to his late adoptive father, now worked as guard. Osamu himself had a small house in Honjo, so that the two brothers lived not far from each other. Besides Osamu, Tamotsu had other relations living in Tokyo or nearby: Yasu, his aunt; her daughters Kei and Sen, both married, one to the owner of a theater tea house and the other to a draper; and Yutaka, still a civil servant, living in Urawa. How much of his aunt and his cousins Tamotsu saw, we are not told; but, one suspects, very little. Yutaka, of course, was as ever a friend.

Within two months of his arrival Tamotsu was registered as a student at three academic institutions. One was a private academy, run by the Chinese scholar and his old mentor, Kaiho Chikkei; one was another private academy, specializing in English instruction, run by a man named Seki Shinhachi (1839–86); and the other was Daigaku Nankō, a government-sponsored college whose curriculum included foreign studies and which later formed part of the new University of Tokyo. In addition, when classes were over at these places of learning, he went for tutoring in English to a Dutch-born American missionary named G. H. F. Verbeck (1830–98). Times had changed, Ōgai reminds us, and Dutch, the language that Tamotsu's father Chūsai had wished him to learn, was no longer the major European language in Japan.

What Tamotsu was doing, then, was to prepare himself for a career in the new society. The study of Chinese medicine, he ceased, presumably for the obvious reason that it would now be useless. The Chinese classics, he would continue to study, for they were an essential part of a liberal education. But most important of all to him was the acquisition of knowledge of the Western world, which had in the course of his lifetime made itself felt in Japan with such overwhelming force.

For all his intelligence, initiative, and dedication to learning, Tamotsu was not to become a major intellectual figure in Meiji Japan. But at least he maintained his family tradition of learning, whether as teacher or journalist, and did gain a measure of distinction in a world where so many men of his background sank into utter obscurity. Perhaps in a sense Kuga was the more impressive person, becoming as she did an acknowledged master of nagauta, though to become so meant the surrender of all claim to gentility, for being a nagauta singer was to be an "entertainer," and thus déclassé (as, of course, being the mistress of a sweet shop was too). One would suppose that she was a less conventional person than Tamotsu, and more forceful. On the other hand, how much more enterprising could one have been than Tamotsu who, at the age of fourteen, left his mother to make a new life for himself and her in the great city, and did succeed in enabling her to live her last years in some comfort, though not exactly in the style she had once been accustomed to?

On the twenty-ninth of August in 1871, the national government at last abolished the domainal system and replaced it with a nationwide prefectural system. This led to the closing down five months later of the domainal mansion where Tamotsu was living.

He moved to his brother's house and stayed there briefly; and in February of 1872 moved into the second floor of a boarding house in a back street by Sumida River in Honjo. The woman who owned it was a forty-two-year-old widow by the name of Suzuki Kiyo. When her husband was still alive the place had been a riverside resthouse that rented boats and entertained customers, but when she became a widow she turned it into a boarding house. It was not a refined establishment, Tamotsu notes, its typical patrons being people of the lower classes.[3] Needless to say he could afford no better, his tuition fees not surprisingly consuming about three-fifths of his stipend. Indeed, it transpires later that he really could not afford even this place, and were it not for the landlady Mrs. Suzuki's infinite patience—for a time he owed her several months' rent—he would have had to find an even humbler one. For many years after he had left there he remembered her kindness and wrote to her. One envies Tamotsu—there seems to have been so much affection in his life, given and received.

Thinking, with good reason surely, that the abolition of the domainal system would mean the relaxation of the policy preventing "desertion of the domain," Tamotsu petitioned the authorities in Hirosaki to permit his mother to come and live with him in Tokyo. The surprising thing is that in spite of the change from domain to prefecture, the local authorities still saw fit to deny Io permission to leave. But this time, the reason given for the denial had at least the semblance of humane consideration, for what they said was that Tamotsu, a mere student, was in no position to provide an adequate home for his mother. And so he asked Yutaka, who was after all respectably employed as a civil servant, to submit a new petition in his name. The petition was successful; and at last, on the twenty-seventh of June in 1872, sixteen months after she and Tamotsu had parted, Io arrived in Tokyo, accompanied by Kuga and her husband Yakawa Bun'ichirō, and Miki. All four settled upon arrival in Mrs. Suzuki's boarding house.

We know nothing about Io's life in Hirosaki after Tamotsu's

departure. The only happening of any note in that time of her loneliness, Ōgai tells us, was that after the former bushi retainers of the Hirosaki domain had been granted parcels of land in partial compensation for the loss of their status, the medical families, now demoted and ranked outside of the gentry, were also given grants of land. The gesture was an afterthought, and the piece of wooded land Io received could hardly have been an "estate." At the time of her departure from Hirosaki, she left the disposition of it in the hands of Asagoe Genryū, the man who had left Edo with her four years before. The Shibue were to receive some additional monetary compensation later (ninety-five *sen* per koku), but that was a pittance.

Honjo, where the boarding house was located, was an area of Tokyo Io knew well, for she had lived there most of her married life, and it was the area the Tsugaru contingent in Edo had been associated with. But her familiarity with Honjo can only have reminded her of better days. No longer the mistress of a large house, she was now a boarder in an establishment which Tamotsu, never a complainer, allowed was not of the best sort.

How large the boarding house was, how cramped their quarters, we have no way of knowing. At least Kuga and her husband did not stay for long, for fairly soon after their arrival she opened her sweet shop. What must have added to the confusion of the ménage at Mrs. Suzuki's, however, was that several months before Io's arrival, Hirano Sadakata, his wife (the one he had married in error, so to speak), and their daughter had ensconced themselves as Tamotsu's guests. Since according to Tamotsu's notes Sadakata and his family stayed with him for about six months, and Io arrived four months or so after he had moved into the boarding house, the two families must have lived under the same roof for a while.[4]

Whether Tamotsu was forewarned of Sadakata's coming, we are not told. What we are told is simply that one day—this was in 1872—he appeared at Tamotsu's lodgings and announced that he intended to be put up there with his wife and daughter, whom he had left behind on the river boat they had all come on. Tamotsu had no choice but to welcome them as his guests, for Sadakata himself would never have thought of doing otherwise had he been in Tamotsu's position. A generous and simple man, he took for granted generosity in those whom he loved and trusted. Indeed, to offer to pay for their room and board, he would have considered an insult to Tamotsu. Nevertheless, while happy to see his uncle, Tamotsu received him and his wife and daughter with some trepidation, if not alarm:

'For though he had promised to pay the widow Suzuki a monthly rent of two ryō, he was so hard up that he had not yet paid her once. He had scarcely enough, as it turned out, to pay for his education. And now he was faced with having to put up three guests. Had they not been who they were, he could have asked them to pay for their room and board. But Sadakata himself had never in his life expected anyone staying in his house to spend a penny of their own money. Tamotsu could hardly be any less hospitable. How he was to support three people in addition to himself, then, was a great worry. Of concern to him too was Sadakata's dignity. There were many people in the neighborhood who remembered Sadakata as the dashing liaison officer of the Tsugaru domain. And now he was forced to seek shelter in this back-street boarding house. Tamotsu found the thought hard to bear.

'Keeping such concerns to himself Tamotsu strove to be as hospitable as he could during the months that they stayed with him. Almost daily he took Sadakata to Owariya, a restaurant in Yokoyama-chō, and treated him to a meal. . . .'⁵

The conjecture is that this Owariya was a branch of a famous eel restaurant of that name. It was clearly not a cheap place, for Tamotsu reports that in time he ran up a bill there of over four hundred yen. Of course he could not afford such extravagance; but, he says helplessly, his uncle deplored the food served at the boarding house, and he did so enjoy being taken out. And apparently it never entered Sadakata's head to think of the money the daily outing was costing his nephew.

By 1872, Sadakata was already a hopeless anachronism. With no head for money, without his horse and his two swords, lacking the learning of even a Yajima Yutaka, he was simply a former minor aristocrat whose values and personal virtues no one now had much use for. The only way he could have prospered in the new society would have been through inheritance of property and of the trappings of status. He had neither. He is hardly a tragic figure; but we can like him, and from this distance admire some of the things he stood for, and be touched by the kindness and love Io's son Tamotsu showed him at the time of his decline.

Sadakata left the boarding house with his wife and daughter when his adopted son Fusanosuke—the one whose adoption Io had objected to—arrived in Tokyo from Hirosaki; and together they moved into a small rented house, again in Honjo. This was probably a little after Io herself had arrived. Later, when Io, Miki, and Tamotsu also had moved into a rented house in Honjo, Sadakata would invariably stop by on his way home from his daily visit to his family temple where his ancestors were buried, and talk with Io, mostly about old times. It would seem that he was not happy in his own house. Once, Tamotsu remembers, he was called there to help his uncle prevent Fusanosuke from covering up the cracks in the walls with old family documents.[6] It is a measure of Sadakata's decline that he, of all people, should have needed another's help to restrain his irreverent adopted son. He died, Ōgai tells us simply, in 1876, aged sixty-four. At the time of his death, Tamotsu notes with sorrow, both he and his mother were in Hamamatsu, a city some 160 miles west of Tokyo, where Tamotsu had been appointed schoolmaster.[7] And so Io lost her foster brother who had always loved her, who had shared with her a time and way of life which now must have seemed to her terribly long gone.

Another person who constantly sought Io's company was her

stepson Yajima Yutaka. At the time of her return to Tokyo he was
a civil servant working for Saitama Prefecture (which had absorbed Urawa Prefecture). He had remained in the town of
Urawa, and so lived close to Tokyo. Now a minor general administrator of the thirteenth rank—the lowest rank being the fifteenth—he was hardly an officer of consequence in the prefectural
government. His salary then, Ōgai tells us, was a mere twenty-
five yen a month, though when supplemented with his travel
allowance (to enable him to visit local offices in the prefecture),
his monthly income came to about seventy yen, which still was
not very much. Nevertheless, it was a time when prefectural bu-
reaucrats were held in some awe by the ordinary folk, and Yutaka
might be considered to have survived rather well. At least he was
respectably employed, which was more than could be said for
Tamotsu and Osamu, who were both still students (Osamu having
lost his job as guard at Lord Tsugaru's mansion), and in no position to supplement what money Io had access to to support
herself and the family, which, one gathers, was dwindling rapidly.

Out of concern for her welfare, then, Yutaka immediately upon
her arrival in Tokyo tried to persuade her to come to Urawa and
live with him, at least for a few years until Tamotsu and Osamu
had completed their education and were able to support her properly. But Io would not listen, saying that she was in perfect health
despite her age—she was then fifty-six—and Yutaka had no need
to worry about her. And so Yutaka had to be content with seeing
her in Tokyo when he could or having her come to Urawa on
short visits. Ōgai writes:

'Whenever he was free Yajima Yutaka would come from Urawa
to inquire after his mother's health. On Saturdays he would come
to take her back to Urawa with him and on Sundays would send
her home on a ricksha. If by any chance he couldn't come to fetch
her himself on a Saturday, he would send a ricksha to Tokyo to
bring her to Urawa.

'The widow Suzuki came to be fond of Yutaka, and would say,
"What a fine, unaffected gentleman he is." In those days Yutaka

sported a beard. It is said that once, when he was presented to Count Kuroda Kiyotaka [the bureaucrat and statesman], a young girl who happened to be there gazed at Yutaka's face for a while and then said, "But his face is upside down!" Though his beard was luxuriant he was thin on top, so that the girl decided the top of his head was his chin. With his beard, formal Western clothes, and a gold watchchain hanging across his waistcoat, it is no wonder that he appeared such a fine gentleman to Mrs. Suzuki.

'One Saturday he appeared at the boarding house at dinner time. So Mrs. Suzuki said to him, "Master from Urawa, will you have dinner?" "Very kind of you," said Yutaka, "but I've already eaten. As I was passing through Akasaka Mitsuke I happened to see a new, rather attractive-looking shop serving tea-over-rice and bean-jam-on-tōfu, so I went in and had two servings of each. Altogether the meal cost me two hundred mon. Very cheap, don't you think?" When she said he was unaffected, the landlady had in mind this kind of assured candor in him.'[8]

We are surprised to be told in passing that Yutaka had actually been remarried in 1871 to a woman named Ōsawa Chō, a daughter of a bushi family. Tamotsu and Io must have met her, but she makes no appearance in the narrative. She was born in 1849, was twenty-two at the time of her marriage, and died in 1882. Of her marriage of over ten years to Yutaka, we are told nothing, except that it was childless.

As for poor Tetsu, we are told only that Yutaka divorced her some time before his second marriage—his brief cohabitation with the antique dealer's wife, we now know was indeed not a marriage—and that soon after arriving in Tokyo with her reluctant guardian Yajima Shūtei, she opened a little toy shop in Honjo. How she fared, or when she died, we simply don't know. One doubts that ever since the death of her parents and her disfigurement in the smallpox epidemic, she had had very many happy days. When Yutaka fled from her and Hirosaki, Tetsu was a shrill, scolding, and terribly embittered wife, and presumably that is how Yutaka, Io, and the others saw and remembered her.

But of course the fact is that she was given little chance to be anything else.

In 1873 Yutaka resigned his post in Saitama Prefecture and returned to Tokyo to work for the Ministry of Industry. In 1875 he was posted to Kyūshū; but soon afterward he resigned from the Ministry, and became a newspaperman in Tokyo, his principal activity being the writing of drama criticism for two small newspapers there. (Osamu, presumably at Yutaka's urging, became a reporter for one of these, the *Sakigake Shinbun*. Io, we gather, was not pleased. Journalism at the lower levels in those days was a suspect occupation; and perhaps not incorrectly, Io feared that working as a reporter for such a newspaper would expose Osamu to bad company.) In 1879 Yutaka again became a civil servant, this time in the Hokkaido Development Office in Sapporo. It was while they were there—in October of 1882—that his wife Chō died. He returned to Tokyo in August of 1883. By then, he was suffering from a weak heart. He moved in with Kuga, telling her that as he was now wifeless, she would have to give up her nagauta teaching and devote her time to housekeeping and to taking care of him. It was rather high-handed of him to impose himself like this on his half-sister. But, Tamotsu says in his defense, he meant no harm.[9]

He did not stay with Kuga long; for on the second of December of the same year, only a few months after his return from Hokkaido, he died. Ōgai writes:

'On the day he died, he had been writing all morning. At about noon he said, "Ah, I'm tired," and lay down. He never got up again. It was thus that this second son of Chūsai, born to Toku, née Okanishi, departed from this world. He was then forty-eight. He had no children. His body was interred in Kannōji, [the Shibue family temple].

'He had been a profligate. But ever since he became a civil servant, albeit of modest rank, he acquitted himself well, showing considerable ability. He was a warm-hearted man, and there were many among his relations and friends who had cause to be grateful to him. He was an accomplished calligrapher, his style showing the influence of Kojima Seisai [Confucian scholar, calligrapher, and Chūsai's friend]. Of his other accomplishments, knowledge of the theater was the most notable; and both he and Mori Kien surely were among the pioneers of drama criticism in modern newspapers. Included in a series published in 1916 by the Society for the Publication of Works of Curiosity is an unfinished piece called "Odd Tales about the Theater." The author, who calls himself "Hichō" [or "flying butterfly"], was in reality Yutaka.'[10]

Not mentioned by Ōgai is Tamotsu's tribute to his half-brother. By the time Yutaka was about thirty, Tamotsu says, he had discarded his earlier bad ways, and was a very good man—honest, steadfast, and considerate. And what Io had done for him seemed always uppermost in his mind. He would say to Tamotsu, "She was incredibly good to me. I can't imagine any real mother who could have been kinder."[11]

A little more than a year before he died, Yutaka changed his surname back to Shibue. The name Yajima that he had had to adopt as a young man could never have had happy associations for him.

We are not told how Yutaka's death in 1883 affected Io. She was sixty-seven at the time. In the following year, she herself was to die.

11 Adjusting to the Modern Age

It was early in 1873 that Io was at last able to move out of Mrs. Suzuki's boarding house and live in a house of her own, again in Honjo. It was rented, of course, and obviously a modest one. By then Tamotsu for financial reasons had left the University and entered Tokyo Normal College on a scholarship, which provided him with a monthly stipend of ten yen a month. Academically it was a step down for him, but the money was needed.

Involved in Tamotsu's admission to the Normal College was Mori Kien, the man once dismissed from service by Lord Abe for behaving so irresponsibly, who in 1872 had returned to Tokyo from Fukuyama, his former lord's castle town (but, in typical fashion, taking several leisurely detours on the way), and became a bureaucrat in the Ministry of Education. He was very fond of Tamotsu, and would constantly visit him at his boarding house and invite him to his own house. He would take him out to nearby eating places, and there, over a cup of sake, would speak with derision of the new society. He was after all a child of old Edo, his lord had been a loyal servant of the Shogunate, and he could hardly be expected to admire all the changes he saw around him.

He lived in a tiny house, built like a shop, standing on a side street. The house had a kitchen, a small room to sleep and eat in, and a front room (if it could be called that) which had no privacy at all, since on entering the house the visitor would immediately

encounter whoever happened to be sitting there, facing the doorway as if waiting for a customer. Tamotsu found him thus on his
first visit to the house, reading at a desk. Taken aback by so sudden
a confrontation with his host, Tamotsu blurted out, "Why, you
look like a fortune-teller set up for business!" Kien burst out
laughing. He was by then sixty-five, but he seems to have retained
much of his earlier carefree nature.

Needless to say, he was not a bureaucrat of high rank. It would
seem, however, that he was not entirely without influence in the
Ministry; for when Tamotsu, on finding that he did not meet the
minimum age requirement for entrance to the Normal College—
he was fifteen, and the requirement was nineteen—mentioned his
difficulty to him, he offered cheerfully to intercede on his behalf.
"That's no problem," he said, "I'll take care of it somehow." With
his help Tamotsu then sent in a petition, and the requirement
was waived.[1] After this brief reappearance Kien takes little part in
the narrative. He died in 1885 at the age of seventy-eight, the year
after Io died. He was without doubt one of the most memorable
of Chūsai's friends.

To supplement Tamotsu's modest stipend as a government
scholar when they moved into their new house, Io took in sewing—understandably without enthusiasm—from a geisha house
she was introduced to by an acquaintance. Living with her in the
small rented house at first were Tamotsu and Miki. But soon
Osamu, suffering from asthma, gave up his own house and moved
in with them. Kuga that year (1873) separated from her husband,
closed down her sweet shop, and became a professional teacher
of nagauta. She lived in her own house.

There is no suggestion that during the two and a half years that
Tamotsu was a student at the Normal College, Io was unhappy.
She had by then become used to poverty, and at least she had her
children close by. For some months she suffered from eye trouble—probably because of the sewing—but otherwise she was
healthy. And what was perhaps most important to her was that
her favorite child Tamotsu was continuing his education—not at

the University, to be sure, but still at a thoroughly respectable institution.

Yet we begin to sense that after her return to Tokyo, Io is not quite her old self. Her mind is unaffected, she does not become querulous; but she is not the commanding figure she once was, and subtly, Ōgai shows her becoming more dependent on Tamotsu.

In January of 1875 Tamotsu graduated from the Normal College, and in the following month was posted to the old castle town of Hamamatsu. There he became a teacher at what was eventually to be called Hamamatsu High School. He was accompanied by Io. Osamu stayed behind in Tokyo and moved in with Kuga. Miki stayed behind too, having the previous year married a dealer in imported goods. Although not the farce her first marriage in Hirosaki had been, this marriage was not to last long either.

After arriving in Hamamatsu mother and son stayed for a while at an ordinary inn. They then moved to another inn, a grander and more comfortable establishment, better suited for a protracted stay. Across the street from this inn was a tavern which they could see from their room. On display outside the tavern was a large platter heaped high with grilled eel fillets on skewers. Tamotsu said to his mother, "Shall I go and get some?" "That would be a terrible extravagance," she said. "I'm sure eel would be too expensive for us even in a town like this." "Let me go and ask," Tamotsu said, and went out. The price turned out to be a mere one sen for five skewers.[2]

Ōgai's comment after he has related this little incident is how cheap things must have been in Hamamatsu in those days. But he intends to tell us more. It is not Io who wants to go and ask the price. She is not just poor, she has become a touch less sure of herself.

At the same time, there is a story told by Tamotsu—but omitted by Ōgai—that shows that Io still had much of her old gumption left. They were apparently so poor at the time Tamotsu was offered the appointment in Hamamatsu that they decided to travel there on foot. On the last day of their journey it rained heavily, and they had no choice but to hire two rickshas. By the time they reached a place called Kakegawa, seventeen miles from Hamamatsu, they had no money left to travel any further by ricksha. Tamotsu sent Io ahead on a ricksha anyway, and himself walked all the way in the pouring rain, anxiously wondering what his mother, utterly penniless, would do about paying the ricksha man when she arrived in Hamamatsu, or how she would fare at the inn. When he at last reached the inn, he was shown to a rather fine room, where he found his mother sitting composedly with the dinner tray set before her. Much surprised by her general air of prosperity and nonchalance, he asked her for an explanation. "Oh," she said, "I simply called the innkeeper as soon as I got here, told him about our circumstances, and asked for a temporary loan of fifteen yen. He gave it to me immediately, and offered to give us more if we needed it." Tamotsu's comment is: "At the time I could only marvel at her self-confidence. But later, in recalling the incident, I thought that the innkeeper's ready kindness and my mother's assumption of it were both characteristic of human relationships in those days."[3]

Their life together in Hamamatsu seems to have been peaceful and comfortable. In time Tamotsu was able to rent a dignified house, in pre-Restoration days the residence of an important retainer of the daimyo of Hamamatsu domain, and situated within the old castle grounds. Perhaps to say their life in Hamamatsu was "comfortable" is not quite true; for Tamotsu, in anticipation of a return to Tokyo for further study, was trying to save as much money out of his monthly salary as possible, and limiting his spending to the bare essentials. But at least they were living in a decent house, and their poverty, which was of the sort we might call "genteel," was of their own choosing.

The sacrifices needed to enable them to return to Tokyo, she must have accepted gladly. High school teaching, for all its respectability—and it was a respected occupation, especially in a small town like Hamamatsu—was not finally what Tamotsu wanted to do, though he was later to return to it. Very well educated in the classics, and now thirsty for modern learning, which in his case meant a good command of English and the knowledge that that would bring, he was satisfied neither with the education he had received at Tokyo Normal College (in Tamotsu's opinion a stodgy and uninspiring institution) nor with the intellectual life he had as a provincial high school teacher. His ambitions, it would seem, were not strictly defined. Simply, whether in politics, in journalism, or in education, he wanted to be a part of the new enlightenment. And Io cannot have wanted any less for Tamotsu.

We have no reason to think that Io was ever a "pushy" mother, with hidebound notions of what constituted success for her children. We know that though a respecter of customs and manners, she was never a conventional person, and was remarkably tolerant. Almost too intellectually curious and certainly too well educated for a woman in the eyes of most of her contemporaries, she seemed to esteem learning for its own sake. (We discover later, for instance, that in her old age she began teaching herself English so that she could read books in that language.) Born rich, she nevertheless or therefore was free of avarice. And though aware of her former place in society, she did not grumble about her loss of it.

What she wanted for Tamotsu, then, was that he should not waste his talents or disappoint himself. It was not likely that he would ever enjoy the prestige that his father had; but Io was much too realistic to expect that he would. Times had changed, and all Tamotsu had inherited as a Shibue was his learning and love of it; that he should be able to preserve at least that with some dignity was her wish.

Of her other children, Kuga was clearly the most talented. And despite the tension one suspects existed between her and her mother, despite Io's greater love for Tamotsu, there is no suggestion that Io felt anything but pride in Kuga's independence and her will to make something of herself. There was no shame in

Io's response to the storyteller's mention of Kuga and her sweet shop. And when Kuga left her husband and set herself up as a teacher of nagauta—she never married again—Io seems not to have shown disapproval. In those days, what Kuga did was a daring thing to do. To leave one's husband and become a single "professional" woman was to give up all claim to gentility. It was not quite like becoming an actress. But her chosen profession put her more or less in the "floating world," that world of professional singers, actors, dancers, restaurateurs, geishas, and so on. It was one thing for a lady to take lessons in nagauta as a hobby; it was another to become a professional at it.

One cannot see Io telling Kuga to become a respectable married woman again. Nor can one see Kuga listening passively to her mother should Io have tried. In Kuga's desire to be a free, self-supporting woman, we see shades of her mother's pride and independence. And if Io in her own lifetime never did anything quite like what Kuga did, it was surely not because she was by nature more conventional, but because she was of a different generation, better protected and more restricted by circumstance.

Io and Tamotsu stayed in Hamamatsu for nearly five years. In 1876, the year after they arrived there, both Io's sister Yasu and her foster brother Sadakata died in Tokyo. Of these two deaths during their absence Tamotsu says simply, "That year, two terribly sad things happened. . . ."[4] Io was then in her sixty-first year.

Presumably because it was uneventful, we are told nothing about her sojourn in Hamamatsu. If she missed Tokyo or if she was lonely sometimes, we are not told so.

In September of 1878 Osamu, who had continued to work as a reporter for the small newspaper in Tokyo that Yutaka was connected with, came to live with his mother and brother. Io had for some time been worried about Osamu's asthma. Besides, having a generally low opinion of reporters working for fly-by-night newspapers, she had been anxious about the sort of company he would be keeping; so that when Tamotsu one day let slip the fact that in a letter to him Osamu had mentioned drinking in the early hours of the morning with his fellow reporters, Io immediately summoned Osamu to Hamamatsu. It would seem that he came willingly enough. The indications are that he was a remarkably malleable person.

By the time of Osamu's departure from Tokyo, his sister Miki had left her husband and joined him in Kuga's house. We are somewhat surprised to learn that the separation was urged by Kuga, who thought very little of her brother-in-law, the imported-goods merchant. Though Io must have been consulted about it, it seems that she had little part in it. She was after all not in Tokyo, and presumably shared Kuga's opinion of Miki's husband. But it is strange, all the same, that in the account we have of the affair, Io should be so much in the background. Perhaps she was tired: we do know that in Tokyo later, some time before she died, her doctor Matsuyama Tōan warned Tamotsu that although she was physically fit, she was suffering from "fatigue of the spirit."[5]

We know so little about Miki that we cannot be certain whether or not she was being too easily swayed by a stronger and more willful sister. It is hard to believe, however, that she left her husband against her better judgment. Also, what we know of Kuga suggests that she was not the sort to meddle unnecessarily in other people's affairs. However strong she may have been, she is described as being a quiet person, not easily moved to tears or anger, and yet having a marvelously bright personality and great wit. Her presence, we are told, always gave pleasure to others. Such is not a description of an interfering busybody. Ōgai obviously liked her very much, and seems to have seen no reason to suspect Kuga's motives in urging Miki to leave her husband.

The two sisters never married again, and died childless. The two brothers did marry and have children, but not before Io died. Io therefore never knew grandchildren.

In October of 1879 Tamotsu resigned from his post at Hamamatsu High School, giving as his reason the continuation of his own education. He had for a long time been wanting to study

English further, and for lack of funds had been unable to do so. Now, having saved a substantial sum of money in the course of his stay in Hamamatsu—at one time, he apparently saved twenty yen out of his salary of thirty yen a month—he was ready to go back to Tokyo, this time to enroll at Keiō Gijuku (now known commonly as Keiō University), a private institution founded by the great proponent of modernization, Fukuzawa Yukichi (1835–1901). A progressive and already distinguished academy, it was probably the ideal place for a liberal young man who wished to study English and Western thought at what was by the standards of the day a sophisticated level. Tamotsu had for some time been an admirer of Fukuzawa, and had even written a short article in his defense when he was attacked by some wilfully misunderstanding reactionary for calling Japan an insignificant country.[6]

By calling Tamotsu "liberal," I mean simply that he was against the centralized, oligarchical government then in power, and was an ardent student of Western democratic institutions and thought. There is nothing contradictory in this young man steeped in the Confucian tradition, son of a classical scholar and a doctor of Chinese medicine, being a child of the new enlightenment. After all, Chūsai, though an adherent of traditional learning, was not obdurately so, and on his deathbed required that his son be taught Dutch, the language which then was the main avenue to Western learning. Besides, his mother, who brought him up, was unprejudiced by nature, always intellectually curious; and being a woman and not a professional scholar, she had no vested interest in the survival of traditional learning, except in so far as it related to personal values and conduct, and to aesthetic matters. And here, Tamotsu gave her no cause for complaint. If he had become so "emancipated" as to ignore her very strict standards of family obligation and filial piety, or if he had shown any inclination to question what she stood for as a well-educated and well-bred woman born a lifetime before the Restoration, or what she stood for as the wife of Chūsai, she would of course have been very angry.

The impression one has of Tamotsu from reading his various accounts of the past is that he was a simple man, reverent and trusting, incapable of condescension toward even what a man like his "uncle" Sadakata, a true product of his time and class, represented. And as a child of Chūsai and Io, he saw himself very much a part of their world, and never betrayed their memory. That at the same time he should have been an adherent of Western learning posed no conflict for him.

In September of 1879, a month before Tamotsu resigned from his post in Hamamatsu, Osamu left for Tokyo to find a house for them. The house he rented—an appropriate one, it would seem, since no complaint is reported—was in Matsumoto-chō in the Shiba district of Tokyo (and so not in Honjo, which had had so many associations for Io). There Io and Tamotsu arrived on the third of November. Io was by now sixty-three, and Tamotsu twenty-two. Miki, then living with Kuga, would come to live with them the following year. Kuga, mistress of her own house, continued to live separately.

The very day after their arrival Tamotsu registered at Keiō. He was unusually well-prepared, so that he advanced rapidly and completed his course of study with an outstanding record in just over a year. While at Keiō he continued his study of English, which, at his level, meant reading and understanding books in English on the history of civilization, law, political economy, and so on. He also attended lectures by authorities on those subjects. Interestingly, the Japanese language, which at that time was in a state of flux as was everything else in Japan, was not neglected in his curriculum either. (The primary problem here was how to express all the new ideas pouring into the country from abroad in a standardized and universally comprehensible language.) What he got at Keiō, then, was what one might call a general modern education, which prepared him to comment with some authority on those aspects of modern civilization and nationhood with which the Japanese in general were most concerned. His earlier classical training could only have enhanced what authority he gained from his attendance at Keiō. One might say that his credentials were ideally suited for modern journalism, which was indeed the profession he went into, though never full-time for long.

His brother Osamu, as ever humble, entered the School of Telegraphy. Training there led to a job in the Post Office, either as a telegrapher or as a clerk. One has to bear in mind that a respectable level of literacy was required in either case, and Osamu was far from being ill-educated.

At about the same time Kuga, while continuing to teach nagauta, began attending Tokyo Musical Academy, which was administered by the Ministry of Education and which taught Western music and music pedagogy. It was later to become Tokyo College of Music, and later still to be absorbed into what is now Tokyo University of the Arts. In other words, it was an institution destined for distinction, and already serious in its purpose.

Tamotsu no doubt would have been happy to continue studying without the distractions of a job. But the money he had so carefully saved while in Hamamatsu was nearly depleted—he had expected it to last much longer—and so when he was offered the position of principal of Aichi Prefectural High School in what is now a part of the city of Toyokawa (190 miles from Tokyo), he accepted. Prior to this there had been talk of his becoming the editor of a daily newspaper about to be started in Mie Prefecture, but Tamotsu withdrew his candidacy when he learned that the paper would receive a subsidy from the prefecture, and thus would not be truly independent of bureaucratic influence.[7]

On the third of August in 1881 Tamotsu left for Toyokawa, accompanied by Io and Miki. Once in Toyokawa they rented a cottage in the grounds of a temple called Chōsenji. Intended as the residence of the retired head priest when there was one, it would have been a dignified and quiet house. It was apparently a spacious one too, for at one time they had six students living with them.

Early in his stay in Toyokawa Tamotsu became a good friend

of one Takeda Junpei, by profession a doctor but more actively engaged in local politics. He had previously been the president of the prefectural assembly, a body composed of local citizens of weight, as distinguished from the bureaucracy, headed by the prefectural governor and appointed by the Ministry of the Interior. This Takeda, while president of the assembly, had a low opinion of the governor, Kunisada Renpei. One year, when the assembly had adjourned, a banquet was held to celebrate the harmonious relationship between the assembly and the bureaucracy. When the banquet was in full swing Takeda left his seat, and sitting down before the governor, courteously poured him a cup of sake. Next he stood up, turned around, and lifting up the skirt of his kimono farted in the governor's face. "Something to go with your drink," he said. He then flung his letter of resignation down on the floor in front of the governor and calmly left the banquet.[8]

At least, this is Tamotsu's version of the incident. Ōgai, having doubts about the delicacy of the story, tells us simply that Takeda lifted up his kimono and presented his bottom to the governor with the apt accompanying remark.

At any rate, we may deduce from either version of the incident that Takeda's feelings against government bureaucracy were very strong. He was otherwise a likeable and affectionate man apparently, and when he and Tamotsu met, they immediately took to each other. Their political opinions were alike, in that they shared a dislike of bureaucracy and the authoritarian central government, and were much in favor of popular rights. They had not known each other long when Takeda proposed that they take vows of fraternity. This would be inappropriate, said Tamotsu, for Takeda was forty-three then and he himself was only twenty-four. So they vowed formally to regard each other as father and son.

Eighteen eighty-one was a year of great political turmoil in Tokyo, when such important parties as the Jiyū-tō (the Liberal Party), the Kaishin-tō (the Progressive Party), and the Teisei-tō (the Constitutional Imperial Party) were in the process of being formed. It was no time, said Takeda, for even those living in backwater places like Toyokawa to remain politically inactive. Tamotsu agreed, and the two formed a political club named Shin-shu-sha (the Progressive Club), with Tamotsu, in recognition of his greater learning, as president and Takeda as vice-president.

What this nascent club might have done, we have no way of knowing, for on the night of January 2, 1882, Takeda was assassinated in his own house. Besides him that day, there were only women in the house. His son-in-law was away in Tokyo, attending medical school; and the living-in students and the manservant had all gone home for the New Year. This is Ōgai's description of the incident:

'That night, after everyone had gone to bed, a fire started in the bathroom. The smell of the smoke woke the one maid who had not gone home. In fright she rushed into the smoke-filled kitchen—the bathroom was just outside of it—and first opening the sky window cried out for help. Takeda immediately came, shouting in response to the maid's call. He was carrying a lantern. A figure, wearing a waterproof cloak, suddenly appeared out of the darkness and approached Takeda. Takeda put down the lantern, and walked away toward the interior of the house. The man in the cloak followed him. They were now in the corridor that ran alongside the inner garden. Takeda kicked open one of the sliding wooden doors pulled shut for the night and went down into the garden. The man still followed him. It was under the cypress tree that Takeda finally fell, with fourteen knife wounds on him.'⁹

It is a sinister scene, described marvelously well by Ōgai. Of all the Japanese writers of his time, he is the true master of terseness.

The police never found out who the assassin was, or why Takeda had been killed. It was the police chief's opinion, however, that the killing was connected with the political club that Takeda and Tamotsu had formed, and he offered to assign two policemen to Tamotsu as personal guards. Tamotsu could not believe that their little club had had anything to do with Takeda's death. But under pressure from others, he agreed to accept the offer of police protection for a while. Io, we are told, now carried her dagger with her at all times, and made sure that Tamotsu had a loaded pistol on him.

Tamotsu believed that Takeda was killed because of some personal grudge, and from what little we know of this apparently incautious man, we are inclined to agree with him. Besides, the so-called political club they had started together could hardly have earned any notice, whether positive or negative, for it could only have been at most a small discussion group, with a few friendly or obliging recruits taking part. In any case, it was soon disbanded after Takeda's death, "not having done anything."

That year Tamotsu became a contributor to the *Tokyo-Yokohama Mainichi Shinbun,* an important newspaper which, when it began in 1870 as the *Yokohama Shinbun,* was the first daily newspaper in Japan. The paper supported Kaishin-tō, the party that espoused popular sovereignty, and it was in that cause that Tamotsu, using his familiarity with English writings on the subject, wrote as a contributor.

By "popular sovereignty," what one means here is "popular male sovereignty." What Io might have thought about women's rights as such, one is not told; nor is it easy to imagine what she might have thought. Perhaps she was born too long before the advent of even limited democracy in Japan to have had any advanced views on the question. That when Tamotsu was writing about voting rights she would have wondered about women, I have little doubt. But there is no way of being sure. In the context of her family or even in the society to which she belonged, she was never meek. But of course that is not the same as the articulation of individual political rights. True, among the men she knew in her prime, there would have been those who felt the outdatedness of the domainal system and the injustices inherent in the hierarchical rigidity of the system, and she too, highly intelligent and trained to think, would have been mindful of other possibilities. Moreover, it would be nonsensical to imagine that

in Hirosaki, both Io and Tamotsu would not have resented the
arbitrariness of domainal authority. But here again, such resentment need not necessarily have translated itself into modern political awareness as a woman on Io's part, even if it did on
Tamotsu's part as a man, especially in his resentment of centralized authority. Of one thing, however, we can be sure; and this
is that within—and often rather beyond—the sphere that by con-
vention she was allowed to operate in, she did not accept inferiority by gender. If this sounds like scant acknowledgment, it is
because we sometimes forget how thoroughly women in nineteenth-century Japan—but why pick Japan?—were indoctrinated
into believing their own inferiority.

In December of 1882, during the school holidays, Tamotsu went up to Tokyo. It was his intention to remain there if he found suitable employment, which indeed he did. He was given appointments at two institutions, Keiō Gijuku and Kōgyokusha, the latter an academy which prepared students for a career in the navy. He was to teach at Keiō in the morning and at Kōgyokusha in the afternoon. His resignation as principal of Aichi Prefectural High School was formerly approved in February of 1883. Then having found a house to rent in Karasumori-chō in the Shiba district, he called his mother and sister Miki to Tokyo. This was in April of 1883.

Kuga continued to teach nagauta in her house in Aioi-chō in Honjo. Osamu still lived with her, and having completed his course in the School of Telegraphy, was now working in the prefectural telegraph office.

In August of that year Tamotsu, having to concentrate on an article he was writing for the *Tokyo-Yokohama Mainichi Shinbun* and needing greater privacy, removed himself from his house and went to stay for a week with a friend living in another part of Tokyo. Miki was in the house in Karasumori-chō to look after their mother; and Kuga, Osamu, and Yutaka (who had just returned from Hokkaido and was living with Kuga) would visit her in his absence.

But Tamotsu was not to have his week without interruption:
'One evening Miki came to tell Tamotsu that their mother seemed unwell and was not eating. Tamotsu immediately went back with Miki, and found his mother in bed.

'"Here I am," said Tamotsu.

'Io smiled and said, "So you've come home."

'"I've been told you aren't eating anything. I myself am going to have some shaved ice, it's so hot tonight."

'"Are you? In that case I'll have some too."

'The next morning, Tamotsu said to his mother, "I think I'll have a raw egg with my breakfast."

'"Will you? In that case, I'll have one too." Io duly ate her egg.

'At noon Tamotsu said to her: "For a change I'm going to order some sashimi and chilled shellfish slices and have that with some sake before lunch."

'"I'll have the same, then," Io said, and had her sake and sashimi with Tamotsu. By this time she seemed her usual self, and was sitting up.

'In the evening Tamotsu said: "When one expects it to be cooler in the evening and it isn't, one seems to feel the heat all the more. Why, there isn't even the hint of a breeze. I shall have a brine bath, and then go to Kogetsu for dinner. It will be cooler there."

'"I'll come with you," Io said. She then had a brine bath too, and accompanied her son to the restaurant.

'Io had stopped eating because Tamotsu had not come home for some days. Of her daughters, she loved Tō most, and of her sons, Tamotsu. When she let her son go to Tokyo and she herself remained in Hirosaki, she bore the long parting because she had made up her mind that it was necessary. But this time, when her son was so near and could have come to see her, she had found the waiting too much to bear. Io was then sixty-seven, and Tamotsu twenty-six.'[1]

Such blatant preference for Tamotsu on Io's part, Ōgai hasn't the heart to chide, although in his repetition of this well-known fact, there is a suggestion of censure, very kindly expressed.

Io was not senile at the time—she never became so—but the signs of aging are clearly there.

Ōgai, a doctor himself, seems to have no doubt that Io's "illness" during her son's absence was psychosomatic. But, for whatever it's worth, Tamotsu does note that Io walked somewhat unsteadily when they went to the restaurant.

It was only four months after this incident that Yutaka died in Kuga's house. Then a little more than two months after that, Io herself died.

'The twenty-sixth year after the death of Chūsai was 1884. On the fourteenth of February of the year, Io died in her house in Karasumori. She was sixty-eight.

'Io throughout her life was hardly ever ill. After Chūsai's death, she once suffered from eye trouble, and occasionally from the colic—that was about all. One might almost say that in her sixties, she enjoyed perfect health—until, that is, the August of the year before her death, when, pining for Tamotsu, she stopped eating. For a time after this, she showed certain signs of weakening of mind and body, which gave her children cause for concern. However, with the coming of the New Year, her condition improved. Tamotsu remembers that on the night of the ninth of February his mother ate some soba noodles topped with tenpura, then covering her legs with a quilt and a foot-warmer at her feet, talked about history with him until the late hours. He remembers too that on the following day, the tenth, she had soba noodles again for lunch. At about three o'clock that afternoon she went out to buy some tobacco. At her children's insistence she had for two or three years now refrained from leaving the house by herself. But because the route from their house to the tobacconist went through the grounds of Karasumori Shrine and therefore was free of traffic, it was the one walk she customarily took alone. Tamotsu was reading in his room at the time, and did not know that she had gone out. After a while she returned, came into Tamotsu's room, and standing behind him started a conversation with him. Wanting to continue with his reading, Tamotsu was only half-attentive to what she said. He was just beginning his study of German then, and the book he was reading was a German grammar. He then became aware that his mother was breathing rather quickly, and said to her, "Mother, you seem a little out of breath."

'She replied, "I suppose when one gets to be my age, even a little walk can affect one like this."

'But she continued talking. Then suddenly Tamotsu noticed that she had stopped. Turning around he said, "Mother, is something the matter?"

'Io was now sitting down by the brazier, her head cocked slightly to one side. Thinking that this was an unusual posture for her he got up and went to her, and looked at her closely.

'Io's eyes stared straight ahead; and out of the corner of her mouth saliva trickled down. Tamotsu cried out, "Mother! Mother!"

'"Yes," she said simply, but otherwise she seemed unaware of her surroundings.

'Tamotsu had her put to bed, then rushed out to get the doctor.

'Close to their house was a clinic called Zonseidō, where Matsuyama Tōan kept a visiting office. Here Tamotsu found the resident doctor by the name of Katakura. A message was sent to Matsuyama, and Tamotsu went back to the house with Katakura.

'By the time Katakura had given Io what preliminary treatment he could, Matsuyama arrived. After examining her Matsuyama said: "It's cerebral apoplexy. Her entire right side is paralyzed. She's hemorrhaged a great deal, and in a very critical area too. There's no hope of recovery, I'm afraid."

'Tamotsu did not want to believe him. Io, who had been staring into space, was now looking at the faces of those sitting around her. When someone left the room, her eyes would follow the departing figure. He saw her reach with her left hand for the handkerchief beside her pillow, and fold it. And each time Tamotsu went close to her, she would even lift her hand and stroke his breast.

'Wanting another opinion, Tamotsu called in a doctor by the

name of Indō Gentoku. He agreed with Matsuyama, saying there
was nothing that could be done for Io.

'At seven o'clock in the morning of the fourteenth, Io at last
died.

'Io's daily life in her late years was remarkably orderly, as though
she were following a printed schedule. Except in times of extreme
cold, she would get up at five in the morning and sweep the
house. She would then wash, say her prayers before the Buddhist
altar, and at six have her breakfast. After that she would read the
newspaper, and then read a book for a while. Next she would
prepare her lunch, which she ate at noon. In the early part of the
afternoon she would do some sewing. At four she would go out
with the maid for her daily walk and a bit of shopping on the
side. This was when she normally bought the fish for dinner. She
had her dinner at seven. After that she would make her entry in
her diary, then read again. Occasionally, when she tired of reading, she would invite Tamotsu to play *go* with her. She went to
bed at ten.

'She had a hot bath every other day, and washed her hair every
Monday. She visited the temple regularly once a month, and ad-
ditionally on the anniversaries of the death of her parents and her
husband. She had managed household expenditures when Chūsai
was alive, and continued to do so until she died. She was an
extraordinarily prudent and skillful manager.

'Of the books Io read in her later years, many were newly published works on history and geography. One book she always had
beside her was *Heiyō Nihon chiri shōshi* [A Concise Geography of
Japan for Military Officers], which she admired for its pithy prose.

'What is astonishing is that Io began reading English after she
had turned sixty. Very early in her life she became curious about
Western learning. Actually, she was younger when she evinced
such curiosity than Chūsai was when he first learned about the
West from Asaka Gonsai's writings. Once, when she was still
living with her brother Eijirō, she heard him telling Sushikyū—
the man whom he had set up as a sushi restaurateur—a very odd
thing, which was something to the effect that at night people

were positioned upside-down on earth. After Sushikyū had left
Io dubiously asked her brother to explain what he meant; and for
the first time she was told about the heliocentric theory.[2] When
later she found *Kikai kanran* [Observing the Physical Universe]
and *Chiri zenshi* [A Complete Guide to Geography][3] lying on her
brother's desk, she took them away and read them.

'After Io and Chūsai got married he once complained to her
about fly droppings on the ceiling. Io replied: "I understand that
at night people are like those flies that cling to the ceiling." We
are told that Chūsai was amazed to learn that his wife was acquainted with the heliocentric theory.

'In her later years Io grew increasingly dissatisfied with Chinese
and Japanese translations of Western works, and finally prevailed
upon Tamotsu to teach her the rudiments of English spelling.
Before long she was reading an English primer; and within a year
or so she was laboriously picking her way through such books as
Parley's *Universal History,* Quackenbos's *American History,* and
Mrs. Fawcett's *Elementary Manual on Political Economy.*'[4]

In this way, then—simply and unsentimentally, quite without
cant—Ōgai takes leave of Io. For him, there could have been no
other way to express his respect for her. And Io herself could not
have wished for any greater tribute.

Io was not in the ordinary sense a distinguished or famous
person; so that had it not been for Ōgai's chance encounter with
her, we would never have known about this remarkable woman,
so brave and so proud.

Io's physical courage is a virtue few people would find difficult
to admire. What makes Ōgai's admiration for her more moving
and persuasive is his capacity to understand another kind of courage in her, the courage which led her to reject Sadakata's offer of
protection against the condescension of others toward widows,
or the courage behind her determination to learn English in her
old age.

At the time of Io's death in 1884, Kuga was thirty-seven, Miki
thirty-one, Osamu thirty, and Tamotsu twenty-seven.

Tamotsu, head of the Shibue house since infancy, lived until

1930. Married at the age of twenty-nine, two years after his mother's death, he had seven children by his wife Matsu. But sadly,
only one of these, a daughter named Otome, was to survive him.
Hardly what one might call a failure, he seemed nevertheless not
quite able to settle down to any one career. Soon after Io died he
became an editor of the *Tokyo-Yokohama Mainichi Shinbun* (with
which he had previously been associated as a contributor), and
in that capacity played an important role in the dissemination of
Western ideas and liberal political views. To students of early
modern Japanese journalism, his name is of some significance. He
was not to remain an editor for long, however. In 1885 he began
to have fainting spells, and following the advice of Matsuyama
Tōan, the doctor who had attended his mother on her deathbed,
he retired to the country for a rest. A few months later he took
up teaching again, this time in a private school in Shizuoka, a city
near Hamamatsu where he had taught previously. In 1888 he
founded his own private school there, called Shibue Academy.

Two years later he returned to Tokyo, and became a translator
and writer for the large publishing house, Hakubunkan. It is a
cruel word to use, but he became in fact a hack for Hakubunkan,
writing and "translating" with enormous speed pseudo-educa-
tional popular works and out-and-out potboilers with such titles
as *Expedition to the North Pole, A Secret History of Russia, The
Essence of Bushidō, A Girl College Student's Penniless Holiday, The
Revenge of the Dead Man, The Curse of the Ghost,* and so on. We
are told that in all he had over a hundred and fifty titles published
by Hakubunkan and its affiliate companies.[5] It is as well that Io
did not live to see her son waste his learning and talent thus.

I think that by nature he was a dedicated student, who would
have been happy, had he had the means, simply to read and learn
all his life, occasionally writing an article of antiquarian interest,
which as a matter of fact he did. Some of the information on pre-
Restoration life and manners which he shared with Ōgai, for
example, he had already published independently as articles in a
journal.

Without him and his memories, we could never have had Ōgai's record of his mother's and father's lives. That Tamotsu loved his mother deeply—too deeply perhaps—there is no question. He once wrote that whenever he visited his parents' grave, he would be overwhelmed with grief as though he were a boy of thirteen.[6] The admission touches us, but there is something a little disturbing about it too. One wonders whether with the passage of time his grief should not have been more contained. One wonders, too, whether after the death of his mother, he did not lose some of his will.

Kuga, his eldest sister, was probably more competent. Not entirely free of antagonism toward her mother, she was, one feels, nevertheless close to her. She had a beautiful singing voice, which Io too is said to have had; she played Japanese chess well, a game at which her mother had excelled, and which the two had often played together; she had also been taught to sew well by her (Io had done most of her own sewing, thinking little of the work of professional seamstresses), and to wield the halberd, and to dress hair in complicated Japanese women's styles. Of all Io's children, it was Kuga who had inherited from her this mixture of tastes and talents, and her will.

As a teacher of nagauta, she won true distinction. Trained by a famous master of the genre, Kineya Katsusaburō, she was given permission by him to start her own studio under the professional name of Kineya Katsuhisa. This was when she was twenty-six, while her mother was still alive. She died in 1921 at the age of seventy-four, after a long and active professional life.

Osamu, though denied the headship of the family despite his seniority over Tamotsu, seems always to have been friendly with his brother. When Tamotsu opened his private academy in Shizuoka, Osamu went there to assist him. He was married while there to a daughter of a prominent local family. He returned to Tokyo in 1890, and for a while taught English. He was back again in Shizuoka before the year's end, working for the national railroad. He was raised to the rank of assistant station master in 1891, but in 1892 we find him in Tokyo once more, this time proof-reading for Shūeisha, one of the large publishing houses. He then had another stint as school teacher in Shizuoka. In 1906 he was back to proofreading in Tokyo, this time for Hakubunkan, his brother's publisher. He died in 1908 at the age of fifty-four. He was survived by three sons, the eldest of whom—Shūkichi—helped Ōgai to get in touch with Tamotsu when he became interested in Shibue Chūsai.

A modest and unambitious man, Osamu probably did as well as he wanted. A sort of camp follower in Hirosaki, an adopted son of a fallen bushi, a minor newspaper reporter, a telegraph operator, a teacher in a private academy, an assistant station master, and finally proofreader for a mass-producing publishing company, his life could hardly be said to have been goal-oriented. But we have the impression that he was a gentle person, and it is comforting to know that he was by no means overlooked by Io, who seemed always to care for him.

We know little about Miki. Married twice unsuccessfully, she seems to have been very dependent on both her mother and sister. As Io's daughter, she cannot have been uncultivated. Possibly she had charm, and possibly she was intelligent; but we really don't know. In 1884, after Io's death, she took her mother's maiden name of Yamanouchi, and set up her own house. She died in 1901 at the age of forty-eight.

Notes

Prologue

1. The main sources for Ōgai's portrayal of Io were a series of documents written or compiled by Shibue Tamotsu and given to Ōgai beginning in November 1915. *Shibue Chūsai* was published serially in the newspapers *Tokyo Nichi Nichi Shinbun* and *Osaka Mainichi Shinbun* from January 13, 1916 until May 17, 1916, and Ōgai was in constant touch with Tamotsu from the time he wrote a rough biography of Chūsai in October 1915 until shortly before he completed the final installment in the middle of May 1916.

The material provided by Tamotsu during the late fall and winter of 1915 took the following forms: a genealogy of the Shibue family (*Shibue kajō*), a chronology of Chūsai's life (*Chūsai nenpu*), and a series of articles being published by Tamotsu in Yamaji Aizan's "small" magazine *Dokuritsu Hyōron*. Of the nineteen articles, published from August 1913 until April 1916, "Kojima Seisai Sensei" (May 1914) and "Daimyo no seikatsu, jō" (July 1914) gave Ōgai crucial insights into Io's upbringing and character. On these and other sources used by Ōgai in writing *Shibue Chūsai*, see Mori Ōgai, *Shibue Chūsai*, ed. Koizumi Kōichirō, in *Mori Ōgai shū* II, vol. 12 of *Nihon kindai bungaku taikei*, intro. by Shigematsu Yasuo, Ogata Tsutomu and Koizumi Kōichirō, eds. (Tokyo: Kadokawa Shoten, 1974), pp. 54–55 nn.4–5, 9–13, p. 525 n.50; Inagaki Tatsurō, "Chūsai botsugo," in *Nihon bungaku kenkyū shiryō sōsho Mori Ōgai shū* II, Nihon bungaku kenkyū shiryō kankōkai (Tokyo: Yūseidō, 1979), pp. 281–83; Ichinohe Tsutomu, "Ōgai saku *Shibue Chūsai* no shiryō," *Bungaku*, 1 (1933), 8, pp. 808–20; Koizumi Kōichirō, *Mori Ōgai ron: jisshō to hihyō* (Tokyo: Meiji Shoin, 1981), pp. 318–20.

In late January 1916, after receiving a biography of Mori Kien (Mori Kien den) written by Tamotsu, Ōgai asked Tamotsu to provide him with accounts of Chūsai's relations and students and a summary of Chūsai's philosophy. Tamotsu complied with the documents *Chūsai shinseki narabi ni monjin* and an appended *Chūsai no gakusetsu*. From these sources Ōgai gained important information about Io's family and Hirano Sadakata, Inagaki Seizō, and Shibue Yasuyoshi (Yutaka). See "Shibue Tamotsu ate," Jan. 24, 1916, letter 662, *Ōgai zenshū,* XXXIII (Tokyo: Iwanami Shoten, 1953), p. 380; Koizumi, pp. 318–19.

That Ōgai determined rather early in his writing of *Shibue Chūsai* to expand it into a chronicle of the Shibue family after Chūsai's death can at least be inferred from the fact that by February 1916, at Ōgai's request, Tamotsu was already writing installments of *Chūsai botsugo,* "a fragmentary, impressionistic, retrospective work in twelve chapters" (Ichinohe, p. 818). Ōgai found the chapters of *Chūsai botsugo* which contained anecdotes about Io to be particularly colorful and interesting. See "Shibue Tamotsu ate," Feb. 14, 16, letters 671, 672, *Ōgai zenshū,* XXXIII, pp. 384–85.

By May 1916, Ōgai was also in correspondence with Io's daughter Kuga (Kineya Katsuhisa). See "Shibue Tamotsu ate," May 6, 1916, letter 720, *Ōgai zenshū,* XXXIII, p. 407. Chapters 113–19 of *Shibue Chūsai* are probably based on an autobiographical essay written by Kuga, though this and her correspondence do not appear to have survived. Ōgai also corresponded with Io's grandson Shibue Shūkichi, who provided him with biographical information about his father, Shibue Osamu.

Ōgai also got in touch with several people who knew of Io. There was, for example, Izawa Megumu, whose father Tōken knew Io in Hirosaki. See diary entries for Mar. 5, May 3 and 5, 1916, *Ōgai zenshū,* XXXII, pp. 149, 160. There was also Nakamura Susumu, whose mother was the cousin of Kuga's former husband, Yakawa Bun'ichirō. See Matsuki Akira, *Shibue Chūsai jinmeishi* (Hirosaki: Tsugaru Shobō, 1981), pp. 95–114.

2. There are two excellent books in English on Ōgai's career: Richard John Bowring, *Mori Ōgai and the Modernization of Japanese Culture* (Cambridge: Cambridge University Press, 1979); and J. Thomas Rimer, *Mori Ōgai* (New York: Twayne Publishers, 1975), Twayne's World Author Series, TWAS 355. Of the various Japanese biographical works on Ōgai I have consulted, two deserve special mention: Mori Junzaburō, *Ōgai Mori Rintarō* (Tokyo: Morikita Shoten, 1942), and Hasegawa Izumi, *Ōgai "Wita sekusuarisu" kō,* 2 vols. (Tokyo: Meiji Shoin, 1968 and 1971).

3. On *Seitō* and Hiratsuka Raichō and the way they were regarded

by the state and the press of the time, see Ide Fumiko, *"Seitō" no onnatachi* (Tokyo: Kaien Shobō, 1975), pp. 45–198. Hiratsuka Raichō never met Ōgai, but in two articles she wrote in 1962, she describes Ōgai's support of the magazine, his involvement with the early women's movement in Japan, and his broadmindedness. See Hiratsuka Raichō, *Hiratsuka Raichō chosaku shū*, VII (Tokyo: Ōtsuki Shobō, 1984), pp. 406–13.

1. *The Early Life and Times of Shibue Chūsai*

1. Only two of Chūsai's works found their way into print during his lifetime: "Yotsu no umi" and *Gotō yōhō*. "Yotsu no umi," a celebratory *nagauta* praising the beneficence of nature and the Emperor, is to be found in Mori Junzaburō, *Kōshōgaku ronkō*, vol. 9 of *Nihon shoshigaku taikei* (Tokyo: Seishōdō Shoten, 1979), pp. 184–85. *Gotō yōhō*, preface dated 1831, is a compilation of the teachings of Chūsai's teacher, Ikeda Keisui (1786–1836), a recognized specialist in the treatment of smallpox.

Keiseki hōkoshi, preface by Kaiho Genbi (Gyoson) dated 1856, was coauthored by Shibue Chūsai and Mori Kien and continues the work of Chūsai's teacher, Kariya Ekisai (1775–1835), in descriptive bibliography. It catalogues, with brief descriptions of location and content, books extant in Japan which were printed in China during the Sung and Yüan Dynasties (960–1369) and in Korea during the Koryŏ Dynasty (918–1392) as well as the various hand-copied versions (*shahon*) of these books made in Japan before the Keichō period (1596–1615). It was first published by the Chinese Embassy in Tokyo in 1885 because it provided a useful means to determine which Chinese texts were extant in Japan that were not extant in China. See Shibue Zenzen (Chūsai) and Mori Risshi (Kien), *Keiseki hōkoshi*, in *Kaidai sōsho* (Tokyo: Kokusho Kankōkai, 1916), pp. 1–171.

A brief review of Chūsai's unpublished work reveals his eclecticism and broad knowledge. Much of his time was spent on the philological study of the *Huang-ti nei-ching* (containing the *Su-wen* and *Ling-shu*), the first systematic description of Chinese medicine, probably compiled in the Han Dynasty (207 B.C.–220 A.D.) and containing countless interpolations in transmission through the centuries. We know of three works he completed in connection with *Huang-ti nei-ching*: *Somon shikishō, Somon kōi*, and *Reisū kōgi*.

Chūsai's less scholarly, and also unpublished, writings include a collection of his Chinese poetry entitled *Chūsai ginkō*, and a record of comments on kabuki actors and other figures in the theater which he heard from his friend Nagashima Gorosaku (Mashiya Gorosaku, or "Gekishinsen"), entitled *Gekishinsen wa.* He is also said to have written a satirical novel based on the life of Empress Lü, the infamous consort of Kao Tsu, the founder of the Han Dynasty.

There is also *Eigo,* a miscellany, which includes a study of the etymology of the compound *hanmon* (agony) in classical Chinese sources, his comments on reading Kariya Ekisai's copy of *Chü lu,* a Sung text on the classification and culture of citrus fruits in Wen province, an etymological study of the compound *nankan* (palsy) in ancient Chinese medical texts, and a study of camels as they appear in classical Chinese texts. On Chūsai's unpublished works, see Mori Ōgai, ed. Koizumi, pp. 148–52, and notes for these; and Mori Junzaburō, *Kōshōgaku ronkō,* pp. 274–93.

2. *Bukan* were not official publications, so that the term *registry* may be misleading. They were privately published directories, begun in the seventeenth century, that listed daimyo, upper-level direct retainers of the Shogunate, and "professional" men such as Chūsai who had been given official recognition by the Shogunal authorities. For each daimyo such information as the following would be given: his lineage, his court rank, the officially assessed rice yield of his domain, the location of his domainal seat and its distance from Edo, his wife's parentage, his designated heir, his crest and other distinguishing emblems, his mansions in Edo, his family temple, the schedule of his required residence in Edo, the names of his senior retainers, and so on. It was obviously a useful publication, and to people with antiquarian interests like Ōgai and Chūsai or to those curious about the great, a source of much pleasure, though from the point of view of the Shogunate somewhat undesirable, for it contained information which the Shogunate, in its autocratic nervousness, would rather not have had made available to the public.

3. At the beginning of the Tokugawa period, both officially and in practice, the doctors retained by the Shogunate, together with Confucian scholars, Buddhist priests, and certain artisans, were regarded as being outside of the social order (*hōgai no to*). Doctors were not regarded as *bushi* (or *shi*), but as men who had abandoned the world. This was to remain the official position of the Shogunate on the status of doctors throughout the Tokugawa period. See Fujikawa Yū, *Fujikawa Yū chosaku shū,* III (Tokyo: Shibunkaku Shuppan, 1980), pp. 29–35. In reality, however, doctors, especially those doctors who were retainers of daimyo in Edo, came to adopt more and more of the symbols of the bushi class: by the Kan'ei period (1624–44), they were using surnames; by 1686, they were wearing short swords with their priestly garb; and by the beginning of the nineteenth century, they were freely using almost all of the ac-

coutrements of the bushi class, including ceremonial swords (Fujikawa, III, pp. 33–42). By Shibue Chūsai's time, domainal doctors in Edo generally enjoyed quasi-bushi status—and in Chūsai's case more than that— their privileges having been gained incrementally over generations. But Chūsai's claim to bushi, or shi, status has to be seen in the context of the relation between the practice of medicine as it was understood in his day and Confucian studies. To understand the difficult classics of Chinese medicine, many of which were compiled during the Han Dynasty, Japanese practitioners of Chinese medicine had to be thoroughly educated Chinese scholars, especially of the Confucian Classics. And it came about that a large number of doctors taught the Confucian Classics in conjunction with their practice of medicine, as Chūsai did. These were known as *jui*, or Confucian doctors. See Hattori Toshirō, *Edo jidai igakushi no kenkyū* (Tokyo: Yoshikawa Kōbunkan, 1978), pp. 23–34; and Anzai Yasuchika, *Nihon jui kenkyū* (Tokyo: Ryūginsha, 1943), pp. 38–43.

It was more as Confucian scholars than as doctors, then, that the jui claimed shi status. The "pure" Confucian scholars, as distinguished from these Confucian doctors, were officially recognized by the Shogunate in Chūsai's time as shi, that is, as not being hōgai no to, or classless persons (Anzai, pp. 41–42). Jui were in a more ambiguous position. But there is no indication that Chūsai himself was ever given reason to think that his status within the domainal hierarchy was not similar to that of the "pure" Confucian scholars.

4. One *koku* of rice, equal to 5.1 U.S. bushels, was the amount of rice held to be necessary to sustain a person for a year. Although Chūsai's official hereditary stipend was 300 koku a year, he did not actually receive 300 koku. At the beginning of the Tokugawa period, the Tsugaru domain granted its retainers fief stipends (*jikata chigyō*), which meant that the individual retainer received the right to tax an area of land assessed as yielding a given amount of koku of rice or something of equivalent value. A bushi receiving a stipend of 1,000 koku, for example, was granted the right to tax an area of land assessed as yielding 1,000 koku. The process of centralization by which the Tsugaru bushi gave up their direct control of their lands, came to live around their lord's castle, and received their stipends in rice from the storehouses of their lord probably began as early as the middle of the seventeenth century, but in 1774 the Tsugaru domain withdrew all fief stipends from the direct control of its retainers and distributed stipends in the form of rice from its own stores.

Even when the retainers of the Tsugaru domain controlled their own fiefs, they could not collect 100 percent of their official stipends; if they did, the peasants on their lands would have starved. Under the new scheme, the percentage of his official koku stipend a Tsugaru retainer living in Tsugaru itself received was about 40 percent. In Tsugaru, retainers similar in status to Chūsai received their stipends in the form of *hyō,* or "sacks," which contained four *to,* a to being approximately one-tenth of a koku; and the number of hyō they received would be the same as the number of koku of their official stipends, so that a retainer whose stipend was 300 koku would receive 300 hyō, or a real income of 40 percent of his koku stipend. Similarly, a Tsugaru retainer living in Edo whose stipend was 300 koku would receive 300 hyō from the domainal storehouse; but the hyō distributed to Tsugaru retainers in Edo contained three to and five *shō* of rice, a shō being one-tenth of a to, so that their real incomes came to about 35 percent of their koku stipends. Expressed simply in terms of koku, then, Chūsai's stipend of 300 koku came to 105 koku of actual income.

Chūsai also received an additional income of ten *fuchi.* Fuchi were generally awarded to retainers for performing certain specific services or for meritorious service. One fuchi was the equivalent of approximately 1.8 koku a year. With his fuchi stipend included, Chūsai probably received an income of about 123 koku a year from the Tsugaru domain. See Hirosakishi-shi hensan iinkai, *Hirosakishi-shi,* I (Tokyo: Meicho Shuppan, 1973), pp. 245–52; and Hirosaki Daigaku kokushi kenkyūkai, *Tsugarushi jiten* (Tokyo: Meicho Shuppan, 1977), pp. 79–81. For the similarity between the system of the Tsugaru domain and that of the Tokugawa Shogunate with respect to its own direct retainers, see Kozo Yamamura, *A Study of Samurai Income and Entrepreneurship* (Cambridge: Harvard University Press, 1974), p. 202 n.27.

Chūsai had substantial income from other sources, but even if we consider merely his direct stipend from the Tsugaru domain, he was securely in the middle of the bushi class, especially in view of the fact that he was not required to be in a state of readiness for war, that is, maintain a horse, armor, firearms, and so on. He was better off than many of the elite bushi directly retained by the Shogunate, the *hatamoto,* and when compared to a low-level bushi or a semi-skilled laborer in Edo, he was quite rich. See Yamamura, p. 13; and Ono Takeo, *Edo bukka jiten,* vol. 6 of *Edo fūzoku zushi* (Tokyo: Tenbōsha, 1979), pp. 112, 115–16, 210–12.

5. In the Battle of Sekigahara which assured the hegemony of the Tokugawa house, the Tsugaru domain headed by Tsugaru Tamenobu sided with the Tokugawa. Tamenobu was subsequently confirmed as chief of his domain which was assessed at 47,000 koku. This figure remained about the same until 1805 when the domain's officially assessed

koku value was raised to 70,000. It was raised again in 1808, to 100,000. This promotion in status, which was all it was, was given in recognition of the domain's undertaking of the defense of Japan's northern islands against the incursions of the Russians. See *Hirosakishi-shi,* I, pp. 805–06; "Nenpyō," p. 83, in ibid.

These figures are meaningful only in that they show Tsugaru's relative status in the hierarchy of domains. In 1688, the domain estimated the taxable value of its own lands at about 260,000 koku; and by Chūsai's time, the real taxable yield of its lands probably came to well over 300,000 koku. See Kodama Kōta and Kitajima Masamoto, eds., *Shinpen monogatari hanshi,* I (Tokyo: Shinjinbutsu Ōraisha, 1975), p. 87; *Tsugarushi jiten,* p. 125.

6. See Jane Bachnick, "Adoption," *Kodansha Encyclopedia of Japan,* I (Tokyo: Kodansha, 1983), pp. 14–15; and Susan B. Hanley and Kozo Yamamura, *Economic and Demographic Change in Preindustrial Japan, 1600–1868* (Princeton: Princeton University Press, 1977), pp. 228–33.

7. *Kōshōgaku* (Chinese: *K'ao-chêng-hsüeh*), or the School of Empirical Research in Confucian Studies (also called the *Han-Hsüeh,* or Han Learning) arose in China at the end of the Ming Dynasty (1368–1644) and continued well into the Ch'ing Dynasty (1622–1911). Opposed to the metaphysical speculations of the Sung and Ming philosophers, this school of scholars called for a return to the earliest extant texts of the Classics, those of the Han Dynasty, and pioneered the development of systematic, empirical scholarship in the fields of phonetics, epigraphy, bibliography, historical geography, and history. See Wm. Theodore de Bary, ed., *Sources of Chinese Tradition,* 4th printing (New York: Columbia University Press, 1960), pp. 612–20; Hellmutt Wilhelm, "Chinese Confucianism on the Eve of the Great Encounter," in Marius B. Jansen, ed., *Changing Japanese Attitudes toward Modernization* (Princeton: Princeton University Press, 1965), pp. 303–07; and "Kōshōgaku/K'ao-chêng-hsüeh," *Ajia rekishi jiten,* III (Tokyo: Heibonsha, 1960), pp. 252–53.

A Chinese school of scholarship that was as important as the *K'ao-chêng-hsüeh* could not but have had an influence on Japanese scholarship as well. It is interesting, however, that the *Kōshōgaku* School in Japan also came to be known as the Eclectic School (*Setchūgakuha*). See "Edo jidai no jugaku," *Nihon rekishi daijiten,* II (Tokyo: Kawade Shobō, 1956), pp. 347–48; and Fujikawa Yū, *Nihon igakushi kōyō,* ed. Ogawa Teizō, I (Tokyo: Heibonsha, 1974), p. 171. Most of the major figures of the Eclectic/Empirical Research School had some direct or indirect association with the Shibue family. Inoue Kinga (1732–84) was the teacher of Taki

Keisan. Yamamoto Hokusan (1752–1812) was the teacher of the merchant Mashiya Gorosaku, whose tales of the theater were recorded by Chūsai. Ōta Kinjō (1765–1825) was the teacher of Kaiho Gyoson and Taki Saitei. Yoshida Kōton (1745–98) was the teacher of Chūsai's teacher, Ichino Meian. See Fujikawa, ed. Ogawa, II, p. 7; and Anzai, pp. 16–17. Kariya Ekisai (1775–1835), a wealthy merchant, seems to have occupied a special place among these doctors and scholars who enjoyed collecting old books, paintings, antiques, old coins, and other things of the past. Ekisai was able to synthesize the various interests of the school—phonetics, epigraphy, bibliography—and make objective, empirical studies of the past that were far more encompassing than the mere textual criticism based on the comparison of varying copies of the same text, which was the scholarly work of most of the other scholars of the school. See Kawase Kazuma, *Zoku Nihon shoshigaku no kenkyū* (Tokyo: Yūshōdō Shoten, 1980), pp. 592–93.

The "eclectic" nature of this school appears to have come about in response to the increasingly acrimonious debates among the major Confucian schools of the time: the Neo-Confucianists, the Yang Ming School, and the Ancient Learning School. To counter these debates, the scholars of the Eclectic/Empirical School attempted to objectively and empirically "blend" (*setchū suru*) the best of the schools under the premise that no matter how extreme the opinion, there was some truth to be found in it. See Anzai, p. 15.

The Shogunate did not look favorably on the kind of intellectual freedom advocated by this school, and in 1790 issued the *Kansei igaku no kin* (Prohibition of Heterodox Doctrines). But what the Shogunate forbade with one hand, it supported with the other: Inoue Kinga, Yoshida Kōton, and Kameda Hōsai all taught the Confucian Classics at the Shogunate-sponsored Seijukan. See Fujikawa, ed. Ogawa, I, p. 218.

The members of the Taki family were the most prominent supporters of empirical textual research in the field of medicine. Chūsai, with his long training in the philological methods of the school, naturally formed a deep friendship with Taki Saitei and aided him in the editing of medical texts. Though the Taki family undertook a great deal of research into classical Chinese and Japanese medical texts, it probably produced no new medical knowledge of practical value. See Fujikawa, III, p. 62; and Fujikawa, ed. Ogawa, II, p. 11.

8. See Fujikawa, III, p. 17; Fujikawa, ed. Ogawa, I, p. 124.

9. See Matsuki Akitomo, "Ahen to Tsugaru ichiryū kintan: Nihon ni okeru keshi saibai no rekishi ni kanren shite," *Tōoku bunka*, 39 (1969).

The Tsugaru house maintained a monopoly over its production by allowing only select medical families of the domain to inherit or receive the "secret formula." In 1816, there were seven such families, three in Edo and four in Hirosaki, the domainal seat. See *Hirosakishi-shi,* I, pp. 440–41.
That this medicine was held in general high regard can be seen by references to it in several kabuki plays. In Kawatake Mokuami's (1816–93) play *Jitsugetsusei Kyōwa seidan* (1878), one of the heroines, Ai, is holding her ill father Sōemon in her arms. A customer in a nearby tea house hears her tearful pleas and offers Sōemon "Tsugaru's *ichiryū kintan,* a medicine that will cure any spasm of pain immediately." See Kawatake Mokuami, *Jitsugetsusei Kyōwa seidan,* in *Mokuami zenshū,* XIV (Tokyo: Shunyōdō, 1934), pp. 224–25.

10. See Stephan Palos, *The Chinese Art of Healing* (New York: Herder and Herder, 1971), p. 80; and Fujikawa, ed. Ogawa, II, pp. 43–45.

11. One gathers that Chūsai did not visit Lord Tsugaru Nobuyuki every day; but presumably Lord Nobuyuki was given a daily examination. We do know that the Tokugawa Shogun was examined by a group of six to ten doctors every morning before breakfast. See Matsudaira Tarō, *Edo jidai seido no kenkyū* (Tokyo: Kashiwa Shobō, 1964), p. 145.

12. A good cultural history of the late Edo period is Nakamura Yukihiko and Nishiyama Matsunosuke, eds., *Bunka ryōran,* vol. 8 of *Nihon bungaku no rekishi* (Tokyo: Kadokawa Shoten, 1967). For an excellent account in English of the literary arts during this period, see Donald Keene, *World within Walls* (New York: Holt, Rinehart and Winston, 1976).

13. Seijukan was originally the private medical academy of the Taki family. It was so successful that in 1791 the Shogunate designated it as its own medical school. Here, under the supervision of the Taki family, medicine was taught purely in the classical Chinese tradition, one of the school's major functions being the editing and publication of classical Chinese texts. Chūsai's being appointed to teach at this school and his friendship with the Taki family were probably the major reasons he was later accorded the honor of being presented to the Shogun. Chūsai is one of nineteen doctors who are listed as having received this honor in the bukan for 1866. See Hattori, pp. 13–14 and p. 783.

14. The post commonly known as "rusui" that was held by Hirano Bunzō and his son Sadakata should not be confused with the post, also called "rusui" and more formally so, held by a retainer of higher rank

who was responsible for the management of the daimyo's residence in his absence. See Kasaya Kazuhiko, "Daimyo rusui kumiai ni okeru gotsū bunsho no shoruikei," *Shiryōkan kenkyū kiyō,* no. 14, pp. 5–6.

Officers occupying the post of rusui referred to here were responsible for maintaining personal contact and correspondence with rusui, or liaison officers, from other domains. This was done within the framework of the *rusui kumiai,* or association of liaison officers. There were several such associations, the membership of each of which was determined by the hall where the liaison officer's lord sat when in attendance at Edo Castle, which again was determined by the size and status of his domain. In other words, the members of a particular association would be officers representing roughly equal domains. See Kasaya Kazuhiko, "Daimyo rusui kumiai no seidoshiteki kōsatsu," *Shirin,* 65, no. 5 (Sept. 1982), pp. 84–85 and 88–89.

These associations appear to have evolved in response to the needs of the domains to coordinate their actions vis-à-vis the Shogunate. Through regular meetings and correspondence, the liaison officers kept one another informed on formal precedents—what gifts to the Shogunate were appropriate on certain special occasions, how many retainers a daimyo should take with him on a journey to a temple, what to do in jurisdictional disputes, and so on.

That these liaison associations were extremely important to the member domains is clear from the fact that large sums of money were provided to liaison officers for the entertainment of other liaison officers. The Shogunate issued edicts ordering the associations to disband, much to the dismay of restaurateurs and brothel-keepers, but such was the importance of these associations that the edicts had little effect. See Kasaya, "Daimyo rusui kumiai . . . kōsatsu," pp. 89–90 and 116–19.

2. The Young Io

1. Mori Ōgai, ed. Koizumi, pp. 98–99.

2. Ibid., pp. 134–36.

3. Ibid., pp. 99–100.

4. The basic economic system of exchange in Tokugawa Japan worked on two tiers: one representation of value was rice and the other was gold, silver, and copper currency. Ideally these two tiers were supposed to complement each other, one gold *ryō* equaling one koku of rice. (On koku see chap. 2, n. 4.) But currency debasement by the Shogunate— the ryō minted in the early 1600s contained about fifteen grams of gold

whereas that minted in the 1860s contained less than two—as well as scarcity or oversupply of rice caused the value of the ryō to fluctuate, sometimes wildly, in relation to a koku of rice. Over the long term, however, one ryō tended to equal one koku. Two other gold currencies besides the ryō which were in wide circulation were the *bu,* which equaled one-fourth of a ryō, and the *shu,* which equaled one-fourth of a bu or one-sixteenth of a ryō. The primary silver currency was the *monme,* sixty monme equaling one ryō. The copper currency was called a *mon.* Six thousand mon equaled one ryō. See Mikio Sumiya and Koji Taira, eds., *An Outline of Japanese Economic History 1603–1940: Major Works and Research Findings* (Tokyo: University of Tokyo Press, 1979), pp. 53–55.

To get an idea of what nine or thirty ryō meant, one could try to determine roughly what a subsistence wage was. At one end of the spectrum, there were probably peasant families that lived on the equivalent of two and a half ryō a year. See Sumiya and Taira, p. 54. People in the more prosperous regions of the country probably made substantially more. Hanley and Yamamura estimate that some unskilled or semi-skilled laborers in Okayama made the equivalent of seven koku a year, and carpenters making three monme a day three hundred days a year earned the equivalent of twelve koku per year. See Hanley and Yamamura, *Economic and Demographic Change in Japan, 1600–1868,* p. 193.

5. Mori Ōgai, ed. Koizumi, pp. 100–07.

6. Ibid., p. 172.

3. The Family and Friends

1. Mori Ōgai, ed. Koizumi, p. 124.

2. Ibid., pp. 109–11.

3. Mori Kien was assigned to work as an editor of the Seijukan printing of a revised Sung version of *Ch'ien-chin yao-fang* compiled by Sun Szu-mo (ca. 581–682 A.D.) from 650 to 659 in T'ang China. *Ch'ien-chin yao-fang* (*Senkin yōhō* in Japanese) is an encyclopedic compendium of clinical practices in thirty volumes with 5,300 entries divided into 230 classifications, and was one of the first medical texts imported from China to Japan to introduce diagnostic methods based on the Yin and Yang and treatment by acupuncture and moxa cauterization. See Mori Ōgai, ed. Koizumi, p. 555 n.273.

4. Ibid., p. 111.

5. Ibid., pp. 176–77.

6. Ibid., pp. 132–33.

7. Ibid., p. 141.

8. *Hsieh-chü chih tao* in Chinese, *kekku no michi* in Japanese. The principle of reciprocity (James Legge's translation) is to be found in the essay "The Great Learning" (*Ta hsüeh*), one of the most important documents in the Confucian tradition. The principle is similar to the Christian one of doing unto others as one would have done to oneself. See James Legge, *The Chinese Classics*, I (Hong Kong: Hong Kong University Press, 1960), pp. 373–74 n.10. Chūsai appears also to have been fond of quoting a line from Han Yü (786–824), "Virtuous men of old were strict in their demands of themselves to the point of severity, lenient in their expectations of others." See Mori Ōgai, ed. Koizumi, p. 590 n.516.

9. Mori Ōgai, ed. Koizumi, pp. 206–07.

10. *Shiji tsugan* (*Tzu-chih t'ung-chien* in Chinese) by Ssu-ma Kuang (1019–87) chronicles 1,362 years of Chinese history in 294 chapters and is considered one of the most reliable of the classical Chinese histories. See de Bary, ed., p. 493.

11. Mori Ōgai, ed. Koizumi, pp. 108–09.

12. As justification for kicking his wife out of the house, Sōemon cites the legend that for three generations male members of Confucius's family divorced their wives. Sōemon mistakenly identifies as the source of this legend K'ung Fu's *Wei-shu K'ung-ts'ung tzu*, when in fact it is *K'ung-tzu chia-yu*. As examples of evil wives, Sōemon cites Chi-chung's daughter, Yung-chi, and the daughter of Saitō Tarōzaemon, both of whom brought about their husbands' deaths through betrayal. In defense of women's honor, Io cites the examples of Chi Ching-chiang, the extraordinarily virtuous mother of Kung-fu Wen-po, and the mother of Yen Chih-t'ui. The reference to Yen Chih-t'ui's mother appears to be a mistake: Io was probably referring to the mother of Chieh Chih-t'ui, who chose to be burned to death with her son, who had incurred the wrath of the Duke of Wen. Io finally defeats Sōemon with a quotation from the poem "Szuch'i" from the *Ta-ya* section of *Shih ching*: "Szu-chi conformed to the example of his ancestors / And their Spirits had no occasion for complaint / Their Spirits had no occasion for dissatisfaction / And his example acted on his wife / Extended to his brethren / And was felt by all the clans and States." See Mori Ōgai, ed. Koizumi, pp. 171 and 478 nn.15–25; and "Szuch'i" in Legge, IV, p. 447.

13. Mori Ōgai, ed. Koizumi, pp. 169–71.

14. Ibid., pp. 196–97.

15. Ibid., p. 136.

16. Ibid., p. 139.

17. On bukan and Chūsai's being presented to the Shogun, see chap. 1, nn. 2 and 13.

18. Mori Ōgai, ed. Koizumi, pp. 114–15.

19. Ibid., p. 114.

20. As we have already surmised (chap. 1, n. 4), the amount of rice income Chūsai received from the Tsugaru domain came to about 123 koku. After taking out of this the equivalent of twenty ryō to pay for the cost of transporting the rice from Hirosaki to Edo (*Tsugarushi jiten,* p. 81) and the amount of rice to be consumed by the Shibue household, Chūsai, who did not like to concern himself with money matters, probably authorized the domain to sell the remaining rice for him. This would have entailed commissions paid both to the domain and the domain's merchant representatives. According to the simple rule of thumb that one ryō equaled one koku, then, the monthly income of five ryō and one bu mentioned by Io—sixty-three ryō a year, sixty-eight ryō in a leap year—seems not unlikely.

21. There seems to be no way of determining with any accuracy what Yamanouchi's income was. A fact omitted by Ōgai but reported by Tamotsu is that through ad hoc "contributions" (*goyōkin*), the Shogunal authorities made off with several hundreds of ryō of the family's money per year. Chūbei would try to hide his gold currency in the garden and under the house and plead a lack of funds, but it would seem that he had little success. The point is that if we don't know what he was worth, it is partly because he had good reason to keep that information to himself.

22. Mori Ōgai, ed. Koizumi, p. 58.

4. Hirano Sadakata, "A True Bushi"

1. Mori Ōgai, ed. Koizumi, p. 107.

2. Ibid., pp. 116–17.

3. Ibid., pp. 118–23.

5. Thieves and Earthquakes

1. On the titular downgrading of the main Date house, the Date of Sendai, and the upgrading of the subsidiary Date house, the Uwajima Date, which was an early supporter of the Imperial cause, see "Dateshi," *Nihon rekishi daijiten,* XII, pp. 192–93; Kaikoku hyaku-nen kinen bunka jigyōkai, *Meiji bunkashi,* I (Tokyo: Yōyōsha, 1955), pp. 399–400.

2. Chūsai's nagauta "Yotsu no umi" is a celebration of the beneficent rule of the Emperor, and, as Ōgai notes, Shibue Tadashige's teacher Shibano Ritsuzan (1736–1807) and Chūsai's teacher Ichino Meian (1765–1826) both expressed their reverence for the Emperor in poems and essays. Ritsuzan, however, was equally respectful of the Shogun, teaching at Shōheikō, the Shogunate-sponsored school, and even helping to author the Prohibition of Heterodox Doctrines (*Kansei igaku no kin*). Ichino Meian was at first a follower of the Neo-Confucian School and an associate of Hayashi Jussai, the official Confucian scholar of the Shogunate. In later years he turned his attention to the editing of Chinese texts based on the methods of the *kōshōgaku* school. The reverence for the Emperor displayed by these scholars was well within the ideological limits set by the Shogunate and should not be confused with the radical advocacy of a return to Imperial rule of such scholars and doctors as Yamada Daini (1725–67), Fujii Umon (1720–67), and Yoshida Shōin (1830–59), all of whom were executed by order of the Shogunate for their beliefs and teachings.

3. Mori Ōgai, ed. Koizumi, pp. 158–61.

4. Some sources place the number of dead in the Great Earthquake of Ansei at over 200,000. See Mori Ōgai, ed. Koizumi, p. 570 n.378. *Kokushi daijiten,* however, places the number at between 7,000 and 10,000. See "Ansei no jishin," *Kokushi daijiten,* I (Tokyo: Yoshikawa Kōbunkan, 1979), p. 384.

5. Mori Ōgai, ed. Koizumi, pp. 133–34.

6. Chūsai's Death

1. The general opinion seems to be that the first outbreak in Japan of cholera (known popularly among commoners at the time as *korori*) was in 1822. It is possible, however, that there were earlier outbreaks of cholera which were not identified as such. In Chūsai's time there was no known treatment for cholera, and it was thus a source of terror for the

population at large. It is estimated that in the 1858 outbreak, 30,000 people died in Edo alone. See *Koji ruien*, XIII, 3rd printing (Tokyo: Yoshikawa Kōbunkan, 1970), pp. 1418–24.

2. Taki Antaku (1822–76) was Taki Saitei's son and was to become Tamotsu's teacher of medicine. Taki Genkitsu (dates unknown) was the youngest brother of Taki Gyōko who was the head of Seijukan, and succeeded Gyōko as head of the Taki family. Izawa Hakken (1810–63) was Izawa Ranken's son and Kariya Ekisai's son-in-law. He was a lecturer at Seijukan, personal physician to Lord Abe Masahiro, and was later personal physician to the Shogun. Yamada Chintei (1808–81) studied medicine at Seijukan, and was a student of both Shibue Tadashige and Chūsai. He was appointed a lecturer at Seijukan later. See Matsuki Akira, *Shibue Chūsai jinmeishi*, p. 290.

3. *Ishinhō*, presented to Emperor En'yū in 984 by its compiler Tanba Yasuyori (912–995), is the oldest extant medical anthology compiled in Japan. It consists of thirty volumes of material drawn from medical texts of T'ang and Sui China, many of which were not extant in China in the nineteenth century.

Chūsai was one of thirteen textual editors appointed to assist in the publication of this "secret" work, inaccessible to the general medical profession for nearly nine hundred years. See Mori Ōgai, ed. Koizumi, pp. 126–28, p. 565 n.344.

4. Kaiho Gyoson (1798–1866) was a renowned scholar of the *Setchūgaku* school. He studied under Ōta Kinjō (1765–1825), a founder of the school in Japan, and was heavily influenced by the textual empiricism of the scholars of the Ch'ing Dynasty. He opened his own private academy in 1830 and was appointed to Seijukan in 1857. A close friend of Chūsai's, he wrote the preface for Chūsai's and Mori Kien's *Keiseki hōkoshi*. Kojima Seisai (1796–1862), also a *Setchūgaku* scholar and friend of Chūsai's, was particularly known for his calligraphy.

Somon (*Su-wen* in Chinese), as one part of the Chinese medical classic *Huang-ti nei-ching*, was indispensable to an understanding of the theoretical foundations of Chinese medicine. See also chap. 1, n. 1.

5. Mori Ōgai, ed. Koizumi, pp. 144–46.

6. Ibid., p. 167.

7. Asaka Gonsai (1791–1860) was a prominent scholar of the Neo-Confucian school, and taught at Seijukan. His special field of interest

was political economy, and his concern about the West stemmed from his desire to reform the Shogunate.

8. *Kanran shuwa* (Talking about Chinese and Dutch Medicine over Drinks of Sake) and *Isseki iwa* (A Night of Talking about Medicine) were written by Itō Kaoru and Hirano Kakkei respectively and argued the superiority of traditional Chinese medicine over "Dutch" medicine that was becoming so fashionable.

9. Mori Ōgai, ed. Koizumi, pp. 161–63.

10. Ibid., pp. 166–67.

11. Ibid., p. 168.

7. Incidents of Widowhood

1. Uehara Gen'ei received an additional six fuchi and Yajima Shūtei an additional eight fuchi. Fuchi incomes have been omitted in the text for simplicity's sake. On fuchi, see chap. 1, n. 4.

2. Mori Ōgai, ed. Koizumi, pp. 175–85.

3. It is interesting that Ono Fukoku (1807–76), a doctor-retainer of the Tsugaru domain based in Edo, was actually a natural grandson of Shibue Honkō, who adopted Chūsai's father Tadashige as heir. Fukoku's father was Reito, Honkō's illegitimate son, who was adopted into the Kojima family. In other words, through this somewhat complicated relationship to the Shibue family, he was invited to take part in the family council.

4. Mori Ōgai, ed. Koizumi, p. 195.

5. Ibid., p. 482 n.22.

6. Ibid., pp. 191–95.

7. Ibid., p. 194 nn.3 and 5.

8. Ibid., p. 185 n.14.

9. Ibid., pp. 184–85.

10. Ibid., p. 605 n.603.

8. The Recall to Hirosaki

1. Ōgai's error is due to Tamotsu's own uncertain grasp of the history

of Tsugaru's shifting allegiances during this period. It must be said, however, that at the time of Io's departure from Edo, the Tsugaru domain was fighting the pro-Shogunate Shōnai domain, and withdrew its troops from Shōnai and joined the anti-Imperial northern alliance only toward the latter part of Io's journey. Then at the very end of August, the pro-Imperial party in Tsugaru, led by Nishidate Kosei, who had rushed back from Kyoto to persuade Lord Tsugaru Tsuguakira to side with the Imperial forces, held sway, and Tsugaru formally declared for the Emperor. Exactly which side Tsugaru was on and when is a matter one could be easily mistaken about. See Inoue Kiyoshi, *Meiji Ishin*, vol. 20 of *Nihon no rekishi* (Tokyo: Chūō Kōronsha, 1966), pp. 111–13; *Shinpen monogatari hanshi*, I, pp. 118–20; *Tsugarushi jiten*, pp. 12–14.

2. Ōgai must be in error about the sequence of places Io and her party passed through, for Yamagata is clearly north of Yonezawa and Itaya.

3. Mori Ōgai, ed. Koizumi, pp. 195–201.

4. Ibid., pp. 611–12 n.642.

9. Life in Hirosaki

1. Mori Ōgai, ed. Koizumi, p. 202.

2. Ibid., p. 615 n.652.

3. Matsuki gives Yakawa Bun'ichirō's year of birth as 1843. See Matsuki Akira, p. 284.

4. Mori Ōgai, ed. Koizumi, p. 173.

5. Ibid., p. 491 n.24.

6. Ibid., p. 208.

7. Ibid., p. 215, and p. 494 n.33.

8. Ibid., p. 619 n.674.

9. Ibid., pp. 208–09, and pp. 212–13.

10. In May of 1868, the new government issued a directive which divided Japan into three categories of administrative units: the *fu,* the *han,* and the *ken.* This was the system known as the *fuhanken sanchisei.* The fu were those major cities formerly under the direct control of the Shogunate, the han (domains) were left under the rule of their respective

daimyo, and the ken (prefectures) were established in areas such as Urawa over which the new government had taken direct control from the Shogunate. In 1871, with the abolition of the domainal system and the end of what autonomy the daimyo had, the fuhanken sanchisei system was also abolished.

A brief look at the history of early Meiji administration of the town of Urawa shows that there were frequent changes in centers of local administration, areas under their jurisdiction, and in upper-level officials. Urawa was first placed under the jurisdiction of Musashi Prefecture in 1868, then a year later was transferred to Ōmiya Prefecture. Toward the end of 1869, Ōmiya Prefecture had its name changed to Urawa Prefecture and the center of administration was moved to Urawa. In 1871, Urawa Prefecture was incorporated into Saitama Prefecture.

The first governor of Urawa Prefecture was Majima Fuyumichi, a man from Owari, the domain of one of the three main Tokugawa houses. Majima was not long in this post before he was transferred to Nagoya Prefecture (Nagoya being the castle town of the Owari Tokugawa) and replaced by Nomura Morihide, who was from Satsuma. See Mori Ōgai, ed. Koizumi, pp. 220–21; Urawashi, ed., *Urawa shisei nijūnen shi* (Urawashi, 1955), pp. 50–51; Tōyama Shigeki, *Kindai Nihon seijishi hikkei* (Tokyo: Iwanami Shoten, 1961), p. 67.

11. Kanematsu Sekkyo studied under Satō Issai at the Shogunate's Shōheikō, then became lecturer in the Classics for the Tsugaru domain (in Hirosaki) in 1835. In 1850, he was ordered to lay the foundations for Western studies in Hirosaki. During the Restoration, he sided with the pro-Imperial faction, and later worked to modernize the domain's educational system, having been appointed supervisor (*tokugaku*) of the domain's official school in 1870. Tamotsu was appointed to teach the Classics by Sekkyo, and perhaps Tamotsu's growing interest in the West was at least in part due to his close association with this learned and humane man. *Hirosakishi-shi*, I, p. 537.

12. Mori Ōgai, ed. Koizumi, pp. 203–04.

13. Ibid., pp. 210–11, and pp. 616–17 n.665–66.

14. Ibid., pp. 213–14.

10. Return to Tokyo

1. Mori Ōgai, ed. Koizumi, p. 216.

2. Ibid., p. 217.

3. Ibid., p. 624 n.701.

4. Ibid., p. 228 n.10, and p. 624 n.701.

5. Ibid., p. 228.

6. Ibid., p. 627 n.715.

7. Ibid., p. 628 n.719.

8. Ibid., pp. 227–28.

9. Ibid., p. 635 n.747.

10. Ibid., p. 246.

11. Ibid., p. 636 n.752.

11. Adjusting to the Modern Age

1. Mori Ōgai, ed. Koizumi, p. 226.

2. Ibid., p. 234.

3. Ibid., p. 627 n.716.

4. Ibid., p. 628 n.720.

5. Ibid., p. 636 n.754.

6. Ibid., p. 503 n.35.

7. Ibid., p. 630 n.734.

8. Ibid., p. 631 n.736.

9. Ibid., pp. 242–43.

12. Io's Last Days

1. Mori Ōgai, ed. Koizumi, pp. 245–46.

2. The heliocentric theory was first widely disseminated in Japan by Motoki Yoshinaga (1735–94), who drew his knowledge from Dutch and Chinese works. Asada Goryū (1734–99), the foremost astronomer of his time, continued to study the astronomical implications of the theory. His disciples participated in the formation of a new calendar, the *Kansei reki*, which was officially adopted by the Shogunate in 1799. See "Chidōsetsu," *Nihon rekishi daijiten*, XII, p. 280.

3. *Kikai kanran* (1825) by Aochi Rinsō (1775–1833) was the first Japanese work on general physics. Aochi was a doctor, a student of Western learning, and a translator from the Dutch and Latin. *Chiri zenshi* (1858) by William Muirhead (1822–1900) was first published in Shanghai in Chinese. Muirhead, who was attached to the London Missionary Society, was born in Edinburgh and lived for fifty-three years as a missionary in China. On *Kikai kanran* see "Aochi Rinsō," *Dai jinmei jiten* (Tokyo: Heibonsha, 1953–55); on *Chiri zenshi* see Kaikoku hyakunen kinen bunka jigyōkai, *Nihonjin no kaigai chishiki* (Tokyo: Kengensha, 1953), pp. 156–58.

4. Mori Ōgai, ed. Koizumi, pp. 246–49.

5. Ibid., p. 260, and p. 641 n.774.

6. Ibid., p. 636 n.754.

Bibliography

Ajia rekishi jiten. 11 vols. Tokyo: Heibonsha, 1959–62.

Anzai Yasuchika. *Nihon jui kenkyū.* Tokyo: Ryūginsha, 1943.

Bowring, Richard John. *Mori Ōgai and the Modernization of Japanese Culture.* Cambridge: Cambridge University Press, 1979.

Dai jinmei jiten. 10 vols. Tokyo: Heibonsha, 1953–55.

de Bary, Wm. Theodore, ed. *Sources of Chinese Tradition.* 4th printing. New York: Columbia University Press, 1963.

Fujikawa Yū. *Fujikawa Yū chosaku shū.* 5 vols. Tokyo: Shibunkaku Shuppan, 1980–82.

———. *Nihon igakushi kōyō.* 2 vols. Ed. Ogawa Teizō. Tokyo: Heibonsha, 1974.

Hanley, Susan B., and Yamamura, Kozo. *Economic and Demographic Change in Preindustrial Japan, 1600–1868.* Princeton: Princeton University Press, 1977.

Hasegawa Izumi. *Ōgai "Wita sekusuarisu" kō.* 2 vols. Tokyo: Meiji Shoin, 1968 and 1971.

Hattori Toshirō. *Edo jidai igakushi no kenkyū.* Tokyo: Yoshikawa Kōbunkan, 1978.

Hiratsuka Raichō. *Hiratsuka Raichō chosaku shū.* 7 vols. Tokyo: Ōtsuki Shobō, 1983–84.

Hirosaki Daigaku kokushi kenkyūkai. *Tsugarushi jiten.* Tokyo: Meicho Shuppan, 1977.

Hirosakishi-shi hensan iinkai. *Hirosakishi-shi.* 2 vols. Tokyo: Meicho Shuppan, 1973.

Ichinohe Tsutomu. "Ōgai saku *Shibue Chūsai* no shiryō." *Bungaku,* 1 (1933), 8.

Ide Fumiko. *"Seitō" no onnatachi.* Tokyo: Kaien Shobō, 1975.

Inagaki Tatsurō. "Chūsai botsugo." In *Mori Ōgai shū* II. *Nihon bungaku kenkyū shiryō sōsho* series. Ed. Nihon bungaku kenkyū shiryō kankōkai. Tokyo: Yūseidō, 1979.

Inoue Kiyoshi. *Meiji Ishin*. Vol. 20 of *Nihon no rekishi*. Tokyo: Chūō Kōronsha, 1966.

Kaikoku hyakunen kinen bunka jigyōkai. *Meiji bunkashi*. 14 vols. Tokyo: Yōyōsha, 1955–57.

———. *Nihonjin no kaigai chishiki*. Tokyo: Kengensha, 1953.

Kasaya Kazuhiko. "Daimyō rusui kumiai ni okeru gotsū bunsho no shoruikei." *Shiryōkan kenkyū kiyō*, no. 14.

———. "Daimyō rusui kumiai no seidoshiteki kōsatsu." *Shirin*. 65, no. 5.

Kawase Kazuma. *Zoku Nihon shoshigaku no kenkyū*. Tokyo: Yūshōdō Shoten, 1980.

Kawatake Mokuami. *Jitsugetsusei Kyōwa seidan*. In vol. 14 of *Mokuami zenshū*. Tokyo: Shunyōdō, 1934.

Keene, Donald. *World within Walls*. New York: Holt, Rinehart and Winston, 1976.

Kodama Kōta, and Kitajima Masamoto, eds. *Shinpen monogatari hansi*. Vol. 1. Tokyo: Shinjinbutsu Ōraisha, 1975.

Kodansha Encyclopedia of Japan. 9 vols. Tokyo: Kodansha, 1983.

Koizumi Kōichirō. *Mori Ōgai ron jisshō to hihyō*. Tokyo: Meiji Shoin, 1981.

Koji ruien. Vol. 13. 3rd printing. Tokyo: Yoshikawa Kōbunkan, 1970.

Kokushi daijiten. 4 vols. Tokyo: Yoshikawa Kōbunkan, 1983.

Legge, James. *The Chinese Classics*. 5 vols. Hong Kong: Hong Kong University Press, 1960.

Matsudaira Tarō. *Edo jidai seido no kenkyū*. Tokyo: Kashiwa Shobō, 1964.

Matsuki Akira. *Shibue Chūsai jinmeishi*. Hirosaki: Tsugaru Shobō, 1981.

Matsuki Akitomo. "Ahen to Tsugaru ichiryū kintan: Nihon ni okeru keshi saibai no rekishi ni kanren shite." *Tōoku bunka*, 39 (1969).

Mori Junzaburō. *Kōshōgaku ronkō*. Vol. 9 of *Nihon shoshigaku taikei*. Tokyo: Seishōdō Shoten, 1979.

———. *Ōgai Mori Rintarō*. Tokyo: Morikita Shoten, 1942.

Mori Ōgai. *Ōgai zenshū*. 35 vols. Tokyo: Iwanami Shoten, 1952–56.

———. *Shibue Chūsai*. Ed. Koizumi Kōichirō. In *Mori Ōgai shū* II. Vol. 12 of *Nihon kindai bungaku taikei*. Intro. by Shigematsu Yasuo. Ogata Tsutomu, and Koizumi Kōichirō, eds. Tokyo: Kadokawa Shoten, 1974.

Mori Ōgai, Ed. Koizumi. See Mori Ōgai. *Shibue Chūsai*.

Nakamura Yukihiko, and Nishiyama Matsunosuke, eds. *Bunka ryōran*. Vol. 8 of *Nihon bungaku no rekishi*. Tokyo: Kadokawa Shoten, 1967.

Nihon rekishi daijiten. 20 vols. Tokyo: Kawade Shobō, 1956–60.

Ōgai zenshū. See Mori Ōgai.

Ono Takeo. *Edo bukka jiten.* Vol. 6 of *Edo fūzoku zushi.* Tokyo: Tenbōsha, 1979.

Palos, Stephan. *The Chinese Art of Healing.* New York: Herder and Herder, 1971.

Rimer, J. Thomas. *Mori Ōgai.* New York: Twayne Publishers, 1975. Twayne's World Author Series, TWAS 355.

Shibue Chūsai. See Shibue Zenzen, and Mori Risshi.

Shibue Zenzen, and Mori Risshi. *Keiseki hōkoshi.* In *Kaidai sōsho.* Tokyo: Kokusho Kankōkai, 1916.

Shinpen monogatari hanshi. See Kodama Kōta, and Kitajima Masamoto, eds.

Sumiya Mikio, and Taira Koji, eds. *An Outline of Japanese Economic History, 1603–1940: Major Works and Research Findings.* Tokyo: University of Tokyo Press, 1979.

Tōyama Shigeki. *Kindai Nihon seijishi hikkei.* Tokyo: Iwanami Shoten, 1961.

Tsugarushi jiten. See Hirosaki Daigaku kokushi kenkyūkai.

Urawashi, ed. *Urawa shisei nijūnen shi.* Urawashi: 1955.

Wilhelm, Hellmutt. "Chinese Confucianism on the Eve of the Great Encounter." In *Changing Japanese Attitudes toward Modernization.* Ed. Marius B. Jansen. Princeton: Princeton University Press, 1965.

Yamamura, Kozo. *A Study of Samurai Income and Entrepreneurship.* Cambridge: Harvard University Press, 1974.

Index

This is principally an index of proper names, but includes a few subject headings, e.g., medicine, domainal stipends, etc. A glossary of selected Japanese terms is incorporated into the index.

Praise for **_Woman in the Crested Kimono_**
_The Life of Shibue Io and Her Family Drawn
from Mori Ōgai's "Shibue Chūsai"_

Edwin McClellan

"Edwin McClellan's book is a superb portrait of a woman living
through the dramatic transition from late Edo to Meiji Japan as well
as a work of distinguished literary and historical scholarship. It illumi-
nates her complex society for a modern reader, beyond the scope of
Mori Ōgai's classic biography."

—Howard Hibbett, emeritus professor of Japanese literature,
Harvard University

"This elegantly crafted book makes quiet but important contributions
to the history of society, of medicine, and of women in the last
century of Tokugawa rule. Professor McClellan has plucked the life
course of an extraordinary woman from Ōgai's biography of her doctor husband, from service in a baronial residence to courageous wife
and quiet household manager. I know of nothing that quite illumines
the social history of its times so well."

—Marius B. Jansen, emeritus professor, Princeton University

"An eloquent evocation of a remarkable woman of nineteenth-century
Japan which seemlessly blends the voices of time: her story recalled
by her children, recounted in Ōgai's historical novel about her husband, and now masterfully reclaimed—and honored—by McClellan
in a tale as spare as it is moving."—Carol Gluck, Columbia University

"The story of the Shibue family, recounted here with enormous skill
and sensitivity by Edwin McClellan, is a uniquely moving record of
what it was like to live through Japan's nineteenth-century upheaval.
Chūsai, his wife Io, his children and family friends are not famous.
They are quite ordinary, which makes their story all the more con-
vincing, all the more accessible, and—paradoxically—all the more
extraordinary. Usually great events are shown through the lives of the
great, but not here. Instead we can see people whose lives are completely disrupted by events beyond their control. Through their experience we are offered a glimpse of what the Meiji Restoration cost
those caught up in it."   —Harold Bolitho, Harvard University